FOUNDATIONS FOR PIAGETIAN EDUCATION

S.H. Jacob

UNIVERSITY
PRESS OF
AMERICA

LANHAM • NEW YORK • LONDON

Copyright © 1984 by

University Press of America,® Inc.

4720 Boston Way
Lanham, MD 20706

3 Henrietta Street
London WC2E 8LU England

Library of Congress Cataloging in Publication Data

Jacob, S. H. 1943-
Foundations for Piagetian education.

Bibliography: p.
Includes index.
Piaget, Jean, 1896-   2. Education—Philosophy.
3. Child development.   4. Cognition in children.
I. Title.
LB775.P49J33   1984   370.1   84-19589
ISBN 0-8191-4327-8 (alk. paper)
ISBN 0-8191-4328-6 (pbk. :   alk. paper)

All University Press of America books are produced on acid-free
paper which exceeds the minimum standards set by the National
Historical Publications and Records Commission.

For Mary, Beth, and Cynthia

Contents

Foreword

The first outline of *Foundations for Piagetian Education* was written in January, 1979 while I was on sabbatic leave in the University of Geneva's Faculte de Psychologie et des Sciences de L'education. I had gone to study and to write about implications of Jean Piaget's work for the educational community.

My first contact with Professor Piaget was an indirect one. He had heard that an educational psychologist had recently arrived who was interested in expanding upon his work on education. He then gave a paper, which he had authored, to the librarian of the Archives de Jean Piaget to give to me. The paper, entitled "ou va l'education?", deepened my conviction that there is a potential educational revolution inherent in Piaget's work. I was convinced then—as I am now—that the present efforts which address educational issues from the Piagetian perspective do so only tangentially. For the most part these efforts constitute introductions to Piagetian psychology with an appendage reserved for educational implications. These introductions are neither *epistemological* in orientation (which is precisely where all of Piaget's work originates), nor are they fundamentally *educational* in focus. H. Furth's (1970) excellent book does not fall into this category. However, it addresses educational issues topically, often leaving the uninitiated reader with a disconnected sense of Piaget's total message for educators.

The present book, like Furth's book, is concerned fundamentally with educational practices which stem directly from Piaget's epistemology rather than from his psychology alone. It is this primary emphasis upon epistemology, the philosophical study of the origin and evolution of knowledge, that can result in a deeper understanding of the impact of Piagetian thought upon the educational world. Therefore, this book is not merely a statement of educational implications stemming from Piaget's psychological theory and its related findings. It is rather an abbreviated version of Piaget's main focus: how the child originates knowledge and how he develops this knowledge. It is out of this fundamentally epistemological concern that the psychology of the child emerges. Piaget's epistemological inquiry led to his psychological discoveries, not vice versa. Accordingly, this book represents a beginning of a theory of education based primarily upon his epistemological theories and secondarily upon his psychological observations.

At the outset, I should point out that Piaget's view of knowing and the knower clashes rather sharply with the view upon which our present system of education rests. The traditional view looks upon the knower as an empty receptable (when newly born) which must be filled with experiences. Experience is defined as an impingement of the environment upon the knower. The knower's role is viewed as passive, responsive, and reactive. To react he needs an external stimulus. To learn, the stimulus must be repeatedly presented, with external reinforcements (rewards) following the response. In short, the knower knows not by virtue of his actions upon reality but by virtue of reality's actions upon his senses. The task of education becomes one of bombarding the students with information, and the criterion for good education is reduced to how efficiently we can impart a predetermined amount of information to the student. Precise reproduction of this information is the ultimate measure of this endeavor. This mechanistic view of man— with its concomitant "laws" of learning—has failed to provide us with a working model of human learners and knowers. One by one these so-called "laws of learning"—generated primarily out of laboratory experiments with white rates and pigeons—are being embarrassed by research into *human* cognitive functioning. One only needs to refer to the recent annual reviews in the field of instructional psychology to appreciate the full meaning of this assertion (see McKeachie, 1974). We must search for viable alternatives, and Piaget's work is one such alternative.

While studying at the Centre*, there were constant reminders of a number of connected ideas which I had previously been convinced could serve as a basis for an educational process that is uniquely human. The most important of these are: intelligence must be viewed as an extension of biological adaptation; knowledge formation is a process which is analogous to the process of epigenesis**; knowledge is actively constructed by the knower and is not a copy of reality; knowlege is therefore personal and pluralistic; the development of all intelligence begins with action; these actions tend to relate their effects to what one already knows; and this relating process, coupled with transformations, manipulations, etc. of the objects of knowledge, results in the knower's final ownership of knowledge.

These ideas construct a view of man-as-knower that is unique in today's world of education. In this framework, man is presumed to be active, curious, investigative, and imaginative. Man wants and needs to know because he must adapt to his surroundings. He adapts by acting on reality and, in so doing, he constructs more complex yet more flexible systems of knowing. He learns most meaningfully by relating the new to the old, the unknown to the known, and by making the new his own. In this way, more elaborate intellectual structures are built. In this framework, "intelligent" is not synonymous with one who knows a lot of facts. Rather, "intelligent" refers to a process of knowing that is characterized by decreasing egocentricity, increasing ability for abstract reasoning, and increasing flexibility in acting, feeling, and thinking. In short, in the Piagetian framework, learning how to learn is more central to the meaning of the term "intelligent" than it is to the term "learning". The latter results in products of knowing, the former in processes of knowing.

I would like to thank Professor B. Inhelder for making my trip to Geneva possible, and to Professors E. Duckworth and M. Bovet for having read and critiqued a paper, later published in the *Educational Forum,* which was expanded into this small book (see Jacob, 1984a; 1984b). I would also like to thank Mary Jacob for her encouragement during the writing of that paper, and Beth Ann Jacob, my daughter, who has confirmed so much of what Piaget has taught me. Finally, I would like to extend my gratitude to my good friends and colleagues, especially Professor William R. Johnson, for their encouragement and critical readings of the manuscript. Obviously, all errors remain my sole responsibility.

*International Center for the Study of Genetic Epistemology, University of Geneva.

**Epigenesis involves four essential features: (a) the process involves a casual sequence of events, (b) it involves increasing differentiation, complexity, and organization, (c) with each step, a new adaptation emerges, and (d) the process involves growth through a series of stages (Kitchener, 1978).

1 Introduction

A number of authors have expressed the view that Jean Piaget is not an educator. For example, Elkind and Flavell (1969, p. xviii) write that: "Piaget views himself as a biologically oriented epistemologist first, a psychologist second, and an educator not at all." Still others have stated that he did not intend to describe a pedagogy, only a theory of cognitive development (e.g., Phillips, 1975). True as these disclaimers may be, it is clear that a basis for a pedagogy is both inherent in Piaget's theoretical position as well as explicit in his writings. In fact his writings on education can be traced back to 1935.

Although these characterizations of Piaget's intentions may be accurate, it is clear that he has made significant contributions to the field of education. More importantly, the educational implications of his theoretical and experimental work have not been fully explored. As to his contributions to education, first, it can be argued that his essays on learning (Piaget, 1959a; 1959b), his work on the factors contributing to cognitive development (e.g., Piaget, 1964) tacitly imply a pedagogical framework. Moreover, the fact that he maintains that the rate of intellectual development can vary depending on maturation, social transmission, physical experience, and equilibration must be considered to be a general statement of the conditions that govern intellectual growth. These writings, then, constitute an implicit foundation for the development of a pedagogy and for a cognitive educational theory.

Moreover, Piaget has also addressed the cognitive aspect of education quite explicitly. His *Science of Education and the Psychology of the Child* (1972a), as well as his more recent publication entitled *To Understand Is To Invent* (1974) bear testimony to that fact. In short, while Piaget's major concern is with the explication of cognitive development itself, it can be shown that he has also addressed himself to the conditions that foster the development of cognition as well. It is the examination and understanding of those conditions that foster the development of cognition that lead to a more formally stated Piagetian pedagogy.

The purpose of this small book is to present Piaget's views on education, with explanation where needed and expansion where possible. It should be said that while this treatment is fundamentally a conceptual one, educational issues will be discussed and practical implications will be drawn wherever and whenever possible. By necessity, the book focuses on the cognitive as opposed to the social or

1

emotive aspects of education. As such, it constitutes a construction of Piaget's contributions to education with a foundation in his theories of genetic epistemology and developmental psychology. This work differs from others because it focuses exclusively on the educational implications and applications of the Piagetian position. In short, I have tried to build a constructivist, or active, view of education, one that is founded on the epistemological, psychological, and educational foundations with which Jean Piaget has left us.

A number of general questions will be explored in the chapters ahead: (a) what are the goals of active education?; (b) what is the nature of the process of knowledge formation?; (c) what are the factors that determine the formation of knowledge?; and (d) how is the process of knowledge formation related to learning and cognitive motivation? Answers to these questions—interwoven with a focus on the development of intelligence through education—finally lead us to the ultimate question: can we create a set of principles upon which we might build an educational style which is compatible with the spontaneous ways in which people construct knowledge?

The first question deals with the goals of education. From the Piagetian perspective, the goals of education must be consonant with the general goals of the society which spells them out. What do we consider important in terms of the general, long-term goals of our educational system? Should the primary goal of education be to transmit our knowledge, our know-how, our art, our music, our values, etc. to our young? Traditionally this has in fact been our educational goal: to teach our young the accumulated wealth of knowledge as well as our values. These laudable goals, however, are unilateral: the society, through its educational system, transmits its knowledge to the young. The society in turn expects the young not only to know what the preceding generations knew but also to transmit this knowledge to the next generation, and so on. On the other hand, we can enunciate goals that are reciprocal, i.e., goals that create an interaction between adult society and its young that goes beyond mere transmission. Society can ask of its young not only to acquire ready-made and handed-down knowledge, but also to enrich it by contributing to its wealth of knowledge. By seizing upon and developing the very natural tendencies of the young to inquire, discover, test, evaluate, search, and invent, society can advance itself. It is not sufficient to transmit our culture's ready-made information to our young. We must enable them to be creative, and to contribute to the intellectual heritage of the culture from which they draw so much. Thus, the fundamental goal of active education is to enable students to become independent thinkers, discoverers, and inventors.

The second question has to do with the origin and development of knowledge. I would like to begin with the claim that active education is not based on intuition or good common sense, rather it is based on systematic study of how learners originate knowledge and how they develop that knowledge. Throughout this book we will be developing the theme that knowledge is constructed by the activities of the knower. That is, learners (knowers) are not born with any preformed or innately given knowledge, nor are they empty receptacles waiting to be filled with experience. Rather, they are equipped with innate mechanisms—their reflexes and their primitive perceptions—to act on the environment, and with coordinations of these actions they build and extend their own intellectual structures. Knowledge is built by an active being. That being is innately curious, manipulative, investigative, etc. Learners are not passive sponges who absorb "experience." Experience is not given to a person, like an injection, or a stimulus. Instead, experience is something the knower creates as he attempts to adapt to a stimulus. In other words, experience is not some stimulus that can be *given* to a subject; it is rather an abstraction that the subject must construct from a certain interaction with an object of knowledge. Reality must always be filtered through the actions of the subject. The result is that the learner is actively adapting to the world around him, creating his own reality. This reality is not the same for all who interact with it: each subject forms his own knowledge of it. Knowledge of ididuals is therefore *personal,* because it has been filtered through their own actions. This point comes to assume some substance when we view the knowledge-forming process developmentally. Consider a variation of a Piaget experiment (Piaget and Inhelder, 1973). A glass of water is placed on a counter top and is shown to a 5 year-old. The child is then asked to examine a drawing that contains four glasses (Figure 1) and point to the one that represents the glass on the counter top. He points to the correct one (Figure 1, *a*). He is then asked to look at the water level of the glass and to draw a line in Figure 1a, showing where the water level is. He does beautifully! He draws the water level parallel to the top of the glass (Figure 2, *a*). The experimenter then tilts the glass of water on the counter top approximately 45° to the right. The child is then asked to point to the glass in the drawing that is positioned in the same way. The child again does beautifully. He chooses the picture in Figure 1, *b*. With the glass of water tilted, the child is asked to draw a line in the picture that he just pointed to that shows the level of the water. Once again, the child draws a line parallel to the top of the glass (Figure 2, *b*), eventhough the real glass of water that he sees in front of him contradicts his drawing. What does this demonstration show? It demonstrates that a stimulus is not merely absorbed by a passive, receiving subject. It demonstrates that the subject is constructing his own reality out of experience. The knowledge that he has constructed is one which had been filtered through his own system of actions. In his view, the level of water is tilted. For him, that *is* reality.

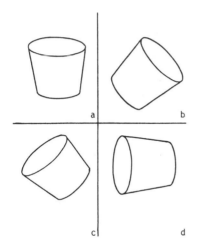

Fig. 1. A drawing
of four glasses.

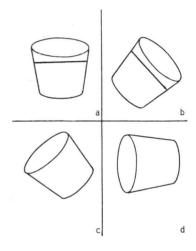

Fig. 2. The child's
drawing of the
water level.

This little demonstration also confirms another critical tenet of developmental constructivism: that this filtering process consists of relating what one is perceiving to the ways of knowing that he has organized for himself. What we "see" is not a copy of what is out there in the world. To a large extent, what we "see" is a function of what we already know. Thus, the famous phrase "seeing is believing" is not always true. In the framework of developmental constructivism, we must always be aware that "believing is seeing." In short, while the empiricists (and today's behavioral psychologists) assume that sensations lead to perceptions which in turn constitute knowledge, Piaget has turned this equation on its head. He has demonstrated over and over again that within the framework of developmental psychology,

4

knowledge determines perception, not the reverse. This "paradigmatic shift," to use T. Kuhn's (1970) phrase, revolutionizes the way in which we view the human learner as well as the learning process itself. The learner is not an empty slate upon which circumstances which happen to him write their fate, nor is he a bundle of nerve tissue which has been preprogrammed by heredity to know the world. Rather, he is instead born with certain innate structures—the primitive perceptual competencies and his reflex actions—from which, and through his actions upon the environment, he constructs his own knowledge. In short, the nature of the learner, of the knower, is that he is a builder of his own intellectual structures.

The third question deals with the factors that influence this knowledge constructing process. To the extent that children share common maturational mechanisms, physical experiences, and socially developed and organized knowledge, to that extent they tend to develop intellectually much the same way. In this way, we can speak of intellectual *stages* which characterize children of certain age spans. Thus, even though each child is a builder of his own intellectual structures, a certain homogeneity in the patterns of thought among children is also evident. Moreover, these patterns of thought tend to be sequentially invariant, suggesting that the *process* of knowledge construction is universally valid. But since builders have to have materials with which to build, and the materials vary from culture to culture, we might expect the *products* of the knowledge construction process to be culturally-specific. Also, because the quality of the factors of maturation, physical experience, and social transmissions differ from child to child and from culture to culture, we can expect children to attain these stages at varying rates of development. Cross-cultural research tends to substantiate these points: that is, while the *sequence* of attaining stages is invariant among children the world over, the *rate* at which these stages are attained can differ from child to child and from culture to culture.

The fourth question relates the developmental process to learning and motivation. We are only too familiar with traditional school learning. The student sits and listens, watches, responds, and carries out directions. The teacher on the other hand reads, prepares, plans, organizes, presents, and evaluates. In general, this is the model that we observe, with exceptions of course. Here the student is the passive recipient of ready-made knowledge. The teacher is the active constructor of her own knowledge. Who is learning more? As any teacher would tell us: if one wants to learn something, then teach it! Bruner (1960) has made this point earlier: teaching is an excellent way of

5

learning. Yet, we strap our learners to their desk and assume that they must be fed ready-made knowledge all at the same time. This model of learning has not changed in centuries. The teacher gives, the student receives. The purpose has implicitly been to educate, and in this context to educate means to enable students to recreate what was fed to them, to repeat society's ready-made knowledge. The model is reminiscent of the behavioristic model of stimulus and response learning. The stimulus evokes a response. This cycle creates a bond between them, an association, which if repeated with sufficient amount and frequency of reinforcement (reward) will lead to more-or-less permanent behavioral changes.

The Piagetian model of learning is diametrically opposed to this conditioning model. For Piaget, the fundamental principle of learning lies in the concept of assimilation, not association. That is, in order to learn some content, one has to relate that content to what he already knows. The tendency to relate what we are now attempting to learn to what we already know is automatic, it is self-regulated. We cannot learn meaningfully unless the new information in some way can be fitted into what we already know. Moreover, learning is limited by the intellectual ways or patterns of knowing, that is, to the processes of knowing of which we are capable. Thus, the relating process must be accomplished through a given intelligence, i.e., through adaptive activity. An example will help to make this point clearer. A child who is trying to learn to multiply can do so if he can relate the process to addition. Children often are subjected to learning the multiplication table without realizing that there is any relationship to something they already know, addition. The child who must "learn" the multiplication table without this assimilatory benefit is at a distinct disadvantage. If he can understand that 5×5 is the equivalent of $5 + 5 + 5 + 5 + 5$, then he is better equipped to learn meaningfully. The child who is not aware of this relationship is learning by rote. He is memorizing. This type of learning, as we all know, is not a lasting one nor can it be transferred to novel situations.

Learning through assimilation is not confined to the realm of mathematics. Adults who have dealt with foreign children (or even adults) will quickly attest to the regular manner in which everything the child (or adult) encounters in the new culture is quickly linked with the old culture: "we used to do it this way." In short, learning rests on assimilation. The second fundamental fact of Piagetian learning is that what we learn must soon become our property, it must be internalized, personalized, and appropriated. This appropriation process takes the form of implementing the new knowledge. "Mommy, look at me" as the child performs some new act is only too familiar. It is critical that the new learning be utilized. It needs to be practiced meaningfully in order for it to be one's own.

The final question involves the construction of an educational scheme that best suits the psychogenetic properties of children. For education to be more than just a trade—to be a profession—it must rest on a solid scientific foundation. In the past, even the best of educational theories were built upon good philosophical intuition or common sense. This is not enough in developing a theory of active education. We must attempt to base our educational theory at least on developmental psychology, the psychology of human learning and cognition, and the psychology of human intelligence. Without this base of knowledge, the teacher cannot understand the students' spontaneous actions. In recent years educators have sought to professionalize education by building a scientific foundation based on the act of teaching itself. Yet educators traditionally have been much too preoccupied with the analysis of teaching, as opposed to the analysis of learning and development. In so doing they have perpetuated the belief that to improve education one must only improve teaching. Although research into comparative methods of teaching has systematically demonstrated that one method is not superior to another, the contention that the improvement of education lies in the improvement of teaching continues among educators.

Since active education de-emphasizes the role of the teacher, particularly as the imparter of knowledge, a shift in what constitutes the solid scientific foundation of education naturally occurs, a shift from the study of teaching to one which bases teaching on genetic psychology and genetic epistemology. As Rousseau, who is perhaps the father of active education, proclaimed: "Begin by studying your pupils, for assuredly you do not know them at all." In the chapters that follow I will be trying to do just that: provide the reader with a concept of learners as Piaget has constructed it. I shall also attempt to demonstrate how learners come to enlarge upon their knowledge as well as what educators have to do in order that they may be responsive to the natural and spontaneous ways in which humans construct their own knowledge.

In summary, I will be emphasizing four main themes throughout this book: the goals of active education, the process of knowledge formation, the factors that determine that process, and the way in which learning and motivation influence development. Given the development of these four themes, I shall then explore a world of education that is consistent with them. It is this educational world which I have called *active* or *constructivist education.*

7

2 The Goals of Education

As we have seen, Piaget views the goals of education in terms of the relation between adult society and the to-be-educated child. He maintains that this relation is unilateral if the goal of education is only to impart society's ready-made knowledge to the child. On the other hand, the relationship between adult society and the child becomes a reciprocal one when

> . . . the child no longer tends to approach the state of adulthood by receiving reason and the rules of right action ready-made, but by achieving them with its own effort and personal experience; in turn, society expects more of its new generations than mere imitation: it expects enrichment (Piaget, 1972a, p. 138).

For Piaget the goal of education should not be restricted to "imparting society's ready-made knowledge to the child." Transmitting a set body of knowledge does not produce people who are creative. To improve society, the goals of education need to exceed mere repetition and imitation. A forward-looking society should stress independent inquiry, discovery, and invention as its ultimate goals for educating its young.

Passivity and Traditional Education

Piaget maintains that traditional education has made the acquisition of a set body of information its primary objective, and it has very naturally chosen to transmit this to students in the most efficient of methods. Since the primary goal of education is the transfer of pre-existing knowledge—knowledge that has been discovered, categorized, and set into words and other symbols—it follows that it must be taught, and taught primarily in verbal form. Classroom learning becomes an exercise in verbal transfer. Teaching (by telling, demonstrating, showing, etc.) becomes central to the educational enterprise and the efficiency of this transfer plays a major role in evaluating both student and teacher. While this is self-evident to any observer of classroom learning, it has been empirically demonstrated that the amount of teacher-talk ("chalk-talk") in the 1960s occupied about 70 percent of classroom time in elementary schools (Bellack, 1966) and that this pattern has not changed since it was first investigated in 1912 by R. Stevens (see Sprinthall and Sprinthall, 1981). Classroom learning is still very much classroom teaching. The impact of this on the student is most ably described by Isaacs (1974, p. 166).

> . . . by [age] seven it [classroom teaching] will usually be waiting for him [student], often already armoured cap-a-pie. He will now form part of a class in a classroom, all called upon to attend, listen and watch, that is, to shut out every other thought and give their whole mind to following careful step by step, wherever the teacher elects to lead.

What's more, traditional educators feel justified in conducting the educational enterprise in this fashion for their view of the learner is consistent with it. As Piaget (1972a, p. 137) has written:

> To educate is to adapt the child to an adult social environment, in other words, to change the individual's psychological constitution in terms of the totality of the collective realities to which the community consciously attributes a certain value. There are, therefore, two terms in the relation constituted by education: on the one hand the growing individual; on the other the social, intellectual, and moral values into which the educator is charged with initiating that individual. The adult, viewing the relationship between these terms from his point of view, began by paying attention solely to the second, and thus by conceiving of education as a mere transmission of collective social values from generation to generation . . . And out of ignorance, . . . the educator concerned himself at first with the ends of education rather than with its techniques, with the finished man rather than with the child and the laws of its development . . . Because of this he was led, implicitly or explicitly to look upon the child either as a little man to be instructed, given morals, and identified as rapidly as possible with its adult models or as the prop of various original sins, that is, as recalcitrant raw material even more in need of reclamation than instruction.

As the above illustrates, the assumption underlying traditional methods is that the learner is raw material to be shaped in "desirable" ways by external contingencies imposed by the school. The learner is viewed as an intellectual sponge who absorbs knowledge imparted to him. This view, which is assumed in all aspects of behavioral psychology, looks upon the learner as a re-active organism, capable of responding to specific stimulus situations, but incapable of initiating and sustaining his own activity without the help of external control. Traditional education consists of methods which reduce the learner's role to passive responding, receiving, memorizing, repeating, etc. Some of the most common instructional methods used today fall under the category of passive methods. For example, programmed instruction, lecture, and audio-visual methods all restrict the role of the learner to reactivity, and at best result in the short-lived memory of some information (Piaget, 1974). In addition, the predominant medium of transmitting knowledge in these methods is language or imagery. Instruction, whether done by the teacher or by a machine, occurs primarily through language. With this frame of reference, the teacher's role in the student's learning becomes paramount! The teacher's functions include: (a) reading, learning, planning, and organizing; (b) continuous directing; where to look, when to act, what to do, etc.; (c) transmitting knowledge; (d) motivating student learning; (e) prescribing content; (f) determining standards of excellence, etc. And all this must be carried out quite efficiently. What's more, the teacher is held "accountable" for the progress or lack of progress of the child.

Given these assumptions, the enthusiasm for performance-based (often erroneously labelled competency-based) education in the U.S.A., with its emphasis on the specification of "terminal behavior" for each student's course of learning, is understandable. Performance-based education, the most popular educational notion today, emphasizes learner objectives stated in behavioral terms, the proper sequencing of these objectives, as well as the careful evaluation of learning outcomes against pre-set criteria of learning outcomes. When the goal, the sequence, the learning activities, and the evaluation of learning are specified by sources external to the student, the initiative for, and the control of, learning shifts away from the student. The current wave of performance-based education is testimony to the fact that we are still enamoured with what the technology of instruction can do to efficiently transmit knowledge. As we have said earlier, when the goal of education is focused on the efficient transmission of information, then the question of the efficacy of one method of passive education as opposed to another becomes a legitimate enterprise. Performance-based education is appropriate, and indeed efficient, in the teaching of specific, ready-made information. However, it is neither consistent with the active intellectual nature of learners nor with the teaching of disciplines which have been discovered or invented by mankind.

Activity and Piagetian Education

For Piaget, (quoted by Duckworth, 1964, p. 5), "the principal goal of education is to create men who are capable of doing new things, not simply repeating what other generations have done—men who are creative, inventive, and discoverers." This is not surprising given Piaget's views on the nature of human intelligence; nor does he claim that such a view is original with him. Piaget (1972a) points out that his educational ideas are consistent with those of Rousseau and his disciple, Pestalozzi, and in turn his disciple, Froebel. Moreover, at least three outstanding American theorists—James, Dewey, and Baldwin—have also influenced Piaget's ideas on education. All of these eminent thinkers have stressed the notion of active, constructivistic learning as opposed to passive, receptive learning. However, the difference between them and Piaget hinges on one fundamental point: Piaget's notion of education rest on a systematic psychology of intellectual development, while prior to him suchpedagogical recommendations were due in large part to the good intuitive sense of these philosophers. Piaget contends that this difference is critical, for without a foundation in the psychology (as well as the sociology) of the child, the practice of education will remain largely intuitive. He insists that education—through a grounding in psychology of development, human learning, and intelligence—can emerge a science. Moreover, he believes that educators can, and indeed they must, turn education into a domain of research-based activity. He maintains that, first and foremost, the goal of education is to help create people who are guided by the active processes of creativity, discovery, and invention.

> The second goal of education is to form minds which can be critical, can verify, and not accept everything they are offered. The great danger today is of slogans, collective opinions, ready-made trends of thought. So we need pupils who are active, who learn early to find out by themselves, partly by their own spontaneous activity and partly through material set up for them; who learn early to tell what is verified and what is simply the first idea to them (Piaget, quoted by Duckworth, 1964, p. 5).

Here we see that Piaget is stressing the processes of independent as well as guided inquiry. As the above quote so clearly states, educators must nourish the act of inquiry that is inherent in their pupils. To do this, educators must provide opportunity for their pupils to question, to experiment, to explore, to manipulate, and in general to search out answers to questions for themselves as opposed to readily accepting them from others. Once again I quote from Piaget (1972a, p. 26):

> If we desire, in answer to what is becoming an increasingly widely felt need, to form individuals capable of inventive thought and of helping the society of tomorrow to achieve progress, then it is clear that an education which is an active discovery of reality is superior to one that consists merely in providing the young with ready-made wills to will with and ready-made truths to know with.

What must be paramount in a theory of constructivistic education, then, is the development of children's natural propensities to explore, discover, inquire, and invent as opposed to the transmission of ready-made bodies of information. Yet traditional education has relied heavily on an aspect of knowledge that makes the imparting of ready-made knowledge efficient: verbal, formalized, symbolically represented knowledge. Often this form of emphasis leads to "empty verbalisms."

Empty Verbalisms: A Major School Problem

Piaget (e.g., 1970) has offered an epistemological distinction between the figurative and operative aspects of knowledge which helps to highlight the differences between traditional and active education in terms of what form of knowledge is stressed. Figurative knowledge refers to acts of intelligence which attempt to mentally represent reality, while operative knowledge refers to intellectual acts which transform such representations. Figurative knowledge refers to the representation of the static aspect of reality, whereas operative knowledge is the mental action which transforms such static states. That is, when we attempt to represent (symbolize, copy, image, memorize, imitate, etc.) reality as it appears to us, without consciously acting to change it, we are basically engaged in figurative knowing; on the other hand, when we act on our representations of reality in an effort to change them, we are then using the operative aspect of our knowledge. Whereas figurative knowledge is derived from acts of perception, imitation, and mental imagery, operative knowledge derives from the individual's spontaneous interactions with the world around him (Piaget, 1970). In short, figurative acts are synonymous with acts of reproduction, while operative acts are synonymous with acts of transformations.

To illustrate, we engage in figurative knowing when we learn specific and set contents of a discipline, as when we learn to spell, learn social conventions, learn chronological order of events, memorize figures, names, dates, etc. Other examples of figurative knowing include attempts to imaginally reconstruct an event, an object, an act, etc. as well as attempts to represent a model's behavior through acts of imitation, or as in learning foreign language pronunciation, or physical exercises and sport moves, etc. On the other hand, we engage in operative knowing when we organize and reorganize these learnings, when we classify our knowledge, when we manipulate ideas, think of alternatives, solve problems, etc.

The distinction can be shown in a number of domains. For illustration, let us use the domain of memory. Children are asked to copy a seriated array of 10 sticks. After 1 week a surprise "test" was given to the children to see what they remembered. Piaget and Inhelder (1973) found that the children's reproductions of the array varied systematically, but only roughly, with the age of the children. Moreover, it was demonstrated that as the younger children grew older, their memories of the array improved! From the standpoint of traditional memory theory, this result is impossible; from the standpoint of genetic psychology, the result is easily explained. In fact, memory of the array does not improve over time, but since the types of transformations that the children could perform change with age, the mental operations that are performed on the static or figurative representation (that is the array) change also. Consequently, older children, who are capable of this type of ordination, view the array as a structure that is logically related: "this stick must be here because it is shorter than that one but longer than this one, etc." Younger children who have not yet developed the capability for such transformations do not reason in this way, as their "reproductions" show.

A number of points relevant to the growth of knowledge can be drawn from this example. First, knowledge does have a figurative aspect and an operative one. Second, the operative aspects transcend the figurative for it is the former that bestows meaning onto the latter, i.e., the intellectual operations of which an individual is capable determines how reality will be perceived. Third, the relative transcendence of the operative over the figurative aspect increases as the child grows, reaching its ultimate with the attainment of formal operations.* This distinction is not a significant one during the sensori-motor stage, because the child's actions are rather limited to his physical manipulations of objects of knowledge. However, by formal operations, possibility transcends reality and therefore the number and variety of *possible* transformations are not reproductions per se or exact copies of the object; rather they are reconstructions, reconstructions that are stage-dependent.

The distinction between figurative and operative knowledge has serious implications for education. Not to recognize this distinction can lead to one of two (or both) equally dangerous educational practices. First, in the act of teaching, the confounding of these two aspects of thought results in a confusion as to what students learn. That is, when we do not recognize this distinction, we may mistake the accumulation of figurative knowledge in our students with the more crucial operative aspect of knowledge. Secondly, equating the figurative with the operative aspect of thought can lead to the teaching of set bodies of knowledge, as an ultimate aim of education. It is the latter problem of which traditional educational methods is particularly guilty. The blurring of the distinction between these two aspects usually results in reducing the operative to the figurative. But as we have seen, it is precisely the opposite—the emphasis on the encouragement of operative acts over figurative ones—that distinguishes active from passive methods of education.

It is not an exaggeration to say that the lack of distinction between the figurative and operative aspects of knowledge is one of our major problems in education. A number of Piaget-oriented educators and psychologists (e.g., Duckworth, 1964; Furth, 1970; Ginsburg and Opper, 1969; Isaacs, 1974; Elkind, 1970, etc.) have spoken out on this very problem: traditional education equates the figurative aspect of knowledge with the operative, often resulting in reducing the latter to the former.

Too often, this reductive fallacy spills over into the realm of language as a symbolic system. This is most clearly evident in the way in which language is viewed in traditional education. That is, traditional education, with its emphasis on verbal learning, has assumed that if a student can represent an object verbally by naming it, defining it, etc., he has acquired a concept of that object. Learning in these cases has been reduced to reproduction or representation. A child who can reproduce or represent an object of knowledge is said to know that object. This type of "concept learning" which has been termed "empty verbalism" by Piaget, and "verbal twilight learning" by N. Isaacs, is primarily the work of imitation and memory. Recently, this notion of concept learning was embellished by advocating that concepts ought to be taught through definitions (sentences) as opposed to names (Markle, 1976). This notion suffers from the same problem: the equation of figurative, representational learning with operative knowing. Elsewhere, I have interpreted Piaget's meaning of "concepts" as consisting not of static representations of reality but of dynamic acts of intelligence that change within the knower as a function of the type of manipulations that may become available to him (Jacob and Deming, 1978).

An example of this type of empty verbalism may be instructive at this point. The fact that a student learns a definition of "homogenization" does not in any way mean that the student has any insight as to the processes involved. Knowing does not consist of the registration of sensory data. The registration of sensory data without an interplay with the operative structures of knowing results in rote learning. Meaningful learning, on the other hand, calls on interactions between sensory data and physical or mental actions carried out on these data; actions that have been, or can be, taken on that data. To be meaningful, the student must relate the term "homogenization" to his experience or abstractions of the process as involved in homogenization. Like any other term, the term homogenization does not have any meaning without a knower (Furth, 1970). Meanings reside in people, not in external objects or in their symbolic (e.g., verbal) representation. This does not mean that symbolic representations (words, definitions, images, imitated acts) are not necessary or useful. Every subject matter has its set body of content that must be mastered. But constructivistic education does not emphasize the development of figurative aspect of knowledge. Constructivistic education offers opportunities for constructing knowledge through activity. Once such activity has been organized, a label may be attached to it. Conversely, when a student inquires about the meaning of a term, it is best to relate the meaning of the term through a set of actions as opposed to through further verbal interchange. In short, constructivistic education offers opportunities for connecting representations with operations and operations with representations (Elkind, Hetzel, and Coe, 1974). Continuing with our example, by visiting a modern dairy one can acquire some knowledge of what is done to milk before it is packaged for commercial use. Through this experience a student may develop a schematization of the processes involved. Here the student may have formulated a more comprehensive conception of homogenization, but he may lack the term that signifies it. Thus, the acquisition of symbolic representations (figurative knowledge) is not sufficient, and it is meaningful only if it represents an operation or a set of operations in the knower. On the other hand, an operation can be meaningful without a symbol representing it. For example, one may know that heating milk at very high temperatures kills the bacteria in milk, but does not know the term (pasteurization) that is usually attached to the process. Thus, while symbols are indispensible in some aspects of knowledge, they are only useful in others.

To return to the example of homogenization, the student's operative knowledge is at an elementary level compared with the plant supervisor's knowledge of the process of homogenization, and the supervisor's knowledge is still qualitatively lower from the industrial chemist's operative knowledge of the same process. Thus,the conceptual level of a given person depends upon his operative knowledge. In all of these cases, the sign ("homogenization") is the same; what changes, from person to person and from one level of comprehension to the next, is the set of transformations that are related to this sign. In short, concepts are personal for they reside within people, not within objects of knowledge. Words represent ways of externalizing (communicating) them, and once words have been linked with operations, then they can be used to internalize those operations. Therefore, language should play a progressively more predominate role in education as we move to the high school years. And even then we must be wary of "empty verbalism" for we cannot assume that the proper operation—word links had been previously established. This is the important point in the distinction between figurative and operative knowledge from the standpoint of teaching: teaching symbols without appropriate operations to which they are linked is to have taught an "empty verbalism." Education must aim at the development of intellectual operations (used broadly) as well as the learning of appropriate symbols to signify these operations. But the accent must always be on operational knowledge. As McNally (1975, pp. 67-68) puts it: "The development of intelligence is therefore primarily a matter of progressive knowing, with figurative knowing playing a subordinate role." It is not surprising then that the active methods of education of which Piaget speaks (and which will be treated in some detail later in this book) are ones whose goals emphasize the promotion of operative knowing over figurative knowledge.

Learning A Set Body of Information

Central as the development of intellectual functions such as exploration, invention, inquiry, and discovery are to the goals of constructivist education, it does not exclude learning through verbal, formalized, representational, forms of knowledge. It may be argued that not all forms of knowledge lend themselves to active discovery and invention, nor do they lend themselves to experimental (cause-effect) or logical (inferential) analysis. What of such knowledge? Must it too be acquired though the processes of manipulation, discovery, and invention? To this Piaget says "no," and he does not deny the importance of such knowledge. He believes that it is just as natural for children to assimilate and memorize names, dates, rules, etc. as it is to spontaneously use their natural inclinations of exploring and discovering, inquiry and inventing.

It is clear from what has been said thus far that Piaget is concerned with fostering the development of independent forms of knowing rather than expediting the learning of ready-made facts. Above all, he emphasizes the spontaneous intellectual activity of the knower. But, it is also clear that thought processes or mental operations must interact with content. Thought cannot be carried out in a vacuum; thinking involves acts of transformation, and transformations must be exercised upon some content. Thus, learning specific content is important in the development of intellect, and Piaget does recognize the need for teaching set bodies of information when he writes:

> Generally speaking, since every discipline must include a certain body of acquired facts as well as the possibility of giving rise to numerous research activities of rediscovery, it is possible to envisage a balance being struck, varying from subject to subject, between the different parts to be played by memorizing and free activity (Piaget, 1972a, p. 78).

This is an important point, for too many have interpreted Piaget's position as one which advocates the use of educational methods of discovery and invention to the exclusion of methods for the teaching of specific content. Not all contents must be acquired through discovery, and not all contents readily lend themselves to inquiry and reinvention. Conversely, and more importantly for our purposes, is the realization that not all contents lend themselves to methods of transmission. Yet, as we have seen, methods of transmission—such as showing, telling, directing, asking short questions which require right or wrong answers—are the most common methods used in our schools today.

Learning Conventional, Discovered, and Invented Knowledge

What we have said thus far implies the existence of a criterion in making decisions as to whether an educator relies primarily on passive methods of knowledge transmission or on active methods of rediscovery or reinvention. Piaget (1972a, p. 26) makes it clear that the historic evolution of a given discipline can give the educator clues as to how best to teach it. Consider the evolution of the subject-matter of spelling. How has it developed? What were the processes which created it and what are the processes of its continual change? The answer points

18

to processes of adult decision-making or collective opinion; a process of numerous individual decisions—over the course of time—that result in accepted *conventions*. And so it is expected that spelling will change as conventions change. By contrast, consider the subject-matter of elementary physics. How has it evolved? Do the processes of individual decision-making predominate, or is there a process more fundamental to the nature of human intelligence? It is clear that the basic principles of physics are not culture-specific nor even culture-sensitive, for its content is not expected to change from culture to culture. And so we see that the principles of physics, unlike those of spelling, are not dependent on the cultural characteristics of the knower of physics. The principles of physics are *discovered* by human-specific forms of intelligence, by the human intellectual endeavor of observation, inquiry, and discovery.

There is still a third manner in which contents of disciplines evolve which we call *invention*. For instance, mathematical truth is neither derived by individual decisions nor is it discovered. Mathematical truth is invented. It is invented by an intelligence common to all mankind. Piaget (1972a, p. 26) expresses it this way:

> . . . there are some subjects, such as French history or spelling, whose contents have been developed, or even invented, by adults, and the transmission of which raises no problems other than those related to recognizing the better or worse information techniques. There are other branches of learning, on the other hand, characterized by a mode of truth that does not depend upon more or less particular events resulting from many individual decisions, but upon a process of research and discovery during the course of which the human intelligence affirms its own existence and its properties of universality and autonomy: a mathematical truth is not dependent upon the contingencies of adult society but upon a rational construction accessible to any healthy intelligence; an elementary truth in physics in verifiable by an experimental process that is similarly not dependent upon collective opinions but upon a rational approach, both inductive and deductive, equally accessible to that same healthy intelligence.

And so we find that the fundamental educational methods of reception, discovery, and invention are all appropriate depending *in part,* upon the content of the discipline. In general, contents which are founded on convention may be taught by methods of transmission, disciplines that are founded on the progressive uncovering of physical properties and their causal interrelations should be taught through rediscovery, and disciplines that are invented are best taught through reinvention.**

The difference between transmission on the one hand, and invention and discovery on the other, may be clear. But what is the distinction between discovery and invention? Piaget states that the difference lies in whether the object of knowledge was there to begin with or not. To use a favorite example of his: the continent which we call America was there prior to Columbus's knowledge of its existence. Columbus uncovered what was already physically there; he did not invent it. The bicycle, however, was invented in that it did not exist as an entity prior to the intelligence which created it. A more subtle example of human invention is our current systems for classifying animals, minerals, or vegetables. Such classifications are abstractions not inherent in these objects themselves, but in our own inventiveness.

Concluding Remarks

In summary, disciplines whose contents are physically present (such as the case with elementary physics and chemistry, astronomy, geology, etc.) lend themselves naturally to some form of rediscovery, guided discovery, etc. On the other hand, disciplines whose contents are abstractions of intelligence itself (e.g., logic, mathematics, certain art forms, etc.) lend themselves naturally to methods of reinvention. In short, rediscovery is appropriate in abstracting properties of objects, while reinvention is appropriate in abstracting properties of thinking itself. These forms of abstraction result from physical experience and are referred to as "simple abstraction" and "logico-mathematical abstraction", respectively.† Another example may be helpful here. According to the genetic epistomology of Piaget, ten rocks are ten not because their physical properties say so, but because the knower says so.‡ Whereas the physical properties of the pepples can be analyzed through acts of discovery, their number is constructed by acts of logic. Finally, disciplines whose content is a matter of collective decision, concensual agreement, and convention are well suited for methods of transmission. Domains in which convention predominate include aspects of language acquisition, such as spelling, vocabulary, punctuation, etc.; some aspects of history; social conventions; typing, etc. For example, it would be unthinkable to teach typing by discovery. The rules developed for the proper execution of this skill are there and they should be efficiently transmitted to students. On the other hand, to learn the rule of "inverting and multiplying" in dividing fractions is perfectly useful but completely meaningless as such. This rule must at least be based on reinventing the general idea that multiplication and division are reciprocal operations.

We conclude that the educator must address himself to his overall goals of education as well as to the nature of the content of the discipline with which he is involved. When the content lends itself to rediscovery or reinvention through active inquiry then such methods ought to be used; otherwise, less active methods of teacher lecture and demonstration, audio-visual presentations, teaching machines, and programmed instruction may be suitable. The following passage further clarified the relation between the goals of education and the question of active versus passive methods of education:

> In cases where it is a matter of acquiring a set body of learning, as in the teaching of languages, the [teaching] machine does seem to be accepted as of undeniable service, especially as a means of saving time. In cases where the ideal is to reinvent a sequence of reasoning, however, as in mathematics, though the machine does not exclude either comprehension or reasoning itself on the student's part, it does channel them in an unfortunate way and excludes the possibility of initiative (Piaget, 1972a, p. 78).

Thus, Piaget does accept the use of passive methods when the goal is the efficient transference of a set body of information from one source (teacher, program, film, etc.) to another (student); however, it can also be seen that he is reluctant to advocate such methods, even in the learning of set bodies of information, for *motivational* reasons. His main contention is that our schools have generally undermined the natural and interactive expression of thought in favor of a verbal learning that is too often artificial and empty of meaning. Other observers of the educational scene have concurred with this conclusion (e.g., Isaacs, 1974, Silberman, 1969; Dennison, 1969). Essentially, the point is that initiative toward rediscovery and reinvention is lost by the first grades of formal education. The initiative which once was spontaneously expressed in the preschool years is no longer evident. Too early in the child's schooling, the initiative shifts: it shifts from self-initiated activity to teacher-directed reactivity, from intrinsically motivated curiosity to extrinsically reinforced obedience. Piaget believes this is so because the process of traditional schooling is contrary to the psychogenetic nature of the knower.

*Piaget has identified four major stages in the process of intellectual development. The formal operational stage is the most complex stage identified. It is characterized by the application of logic in the solution of physical problems and logico-mathematical truths. Sensorimotor intelligence represents the first step in this process of epiginesis in which the baby knows solely by applying his sensory mechanisms and primitive perceptiong in an effort to know an object. A brief discussion of the various stages appears in Chapter 3.

**It should be noted that Piaget's concept of constructivism, as we shall see shortly, emphasizes an element of activity (construction) even in the acquisition of "conventionally" set bodies of knowledge. Thus, from the standpoint of genetic epistemology, all knowledge is constructed.

†This distinction will be discussed in detail in a later section of this book.

‡Once again this argument can only be understood from the standpoint of the psychogenetic nature of knowledge formation, viz., a 3 year-old does not recognize that the 10 rocks that we label 10 is indeed 10.

3 The Formation of Knowledge

Earlier I pointed out that Piaget's emphasis on methods of activity which highlight inquiry, discovery, and invention is not new. A number of philosophers concerned with educational issues have made a similar point. But I also pointed out that the factor which distinguishes Piaget's position from theirs is a systematic psychogenetic study which revitalizes the theme of activity learning by providing a new and much needed psychological footing. The combined result, as exemplified by today's English infant schools, is a fresh educational approach. Obviously, it is not possible to reconstruct Piaget's psychogenetic study of the growth of knowledge; we can only hope to outline some central issues that relate to education here.

The Formation of Knowledge

In his *Principles of Genetic Epistemology,* Piaget (1972b) distinguishes three philosophical (more precisely epistemological) positions on the problem of the formation of knowledge. What follows is a thumbnail sketch of each of these positions.

NATIVISM

First, there exists the point of view known as *innatist,* that posits the *pre*formation of knowledge in the form of hereditary codes. According to this view, knowledge is preprogrammed in individuals and this programming exists prior to any experience or learning. Since knowledge structures are already established prior to any experience, experience is necessary only as a releasing mechanism for what was already determined by heredity. Whereas heredity determines the type of knowledge of which one becomes capable, maturation determines the rate at which this knowledge manifests itself. This is to say that knowledge structures do not evolve in time as a result of interaction with the world (experience); rather, they are already established prior to any experience. The argument continues stating that these innate stuctures enable us to adapt to the world around us, and, of course, this adaptation gradually leads to such universal ways of knowing as the ability to conduct experiments and to reason logically.

A number of psychological theories adhere to the innatist viewpoint, among them the developmental theory of Arnold Gesell; the Gestalt psychology of Kohler, Wertheimer and others; the psycholinguistic theory of Noam Chomsky; and the hypothesis of the heritability of intelligence of Arthur Jensen. There are others, of course, who are closely associated with the innatist position, foremost among them Konrad Lorenz. In all of these cases, it is assumed that behavior has its antecedents in genetic programming. To illustrate the innatist viewpoint, the theories of Chomsky will be briefly mentioned.

Chomsky's (1965, 1972) theory is based on the premise that human linguistic competence (as opposed to performance) is inborn, that human language structures have their origin in heredity. His theory purports to unviel the principles of a universal grammar which underlies all nonartificial human language. In support of his theory, Chomsky presents evidence based on spontaneous utterances of children around the world. For example, linguistic errors which are committed by native speakers as they try to learn their own language show remarkably similar patterns. For example, English speaking children often transform the present tense to past tense by adding "ed" at the end of words even when the rule results in words that the children have never heard: "I sitted down and I holded on." More convincing evidence derives from the fact that children—as well as adults—continue to utter grammatically correct yet novel sentences in most cases without being able to articulate the rules used to generate them, and in all cases without stopping to "diagram" their sentences. Chomsky argues that we so perform by virtue of the underlying structure with which we are innately equipped. That is, our preformed linguistic structure (our underlying competence) enables us to generate novel yet grammatically correct sentences (performance). The relation between competence and performance is rule-governed. The grammatical possibilities follow specific and highly limited rules which are governed by heredity. The task is to pinpoint the specific rules of grammar which govern all human language. For example, the relation which binds subject and predicate may be so fixed as to enable people to produce sentences that are grammatically invariant. It has been claimed that such invariant relations exist across all human languages, which would tend to support Chomsky's hypothesis of "universal grammar." Furthermore, such universality is compelling in leading Chomsky to speak of innately organized linguistic structures.

EMPIRICISM

A second position, which emphasizes the role of experience over heredity, known as the *empiricist* view, holds that it is through experi-

24

ence that we form knowledge. In effect, what we know is fundamentally dependent on what we have experienced. In this view, the relationship between the subject (knower) and the object of knowledge (known) is unilateral: the object gives and the subject receives. In the end, the subject's knowledge is an accumulation of his past experiences. Emphasizing the significance of experience over the internal capabilities of the subject is a version of the empiricist view better known as behaviorism. A basic contention of behaviorists is that it is through experience with the environment that we discover its properties. We learn about the environment thrugh our senses. We learn by responding, reacting, repeating, trying and failing, trying and succeeding. The empiricist view is one which subordinates the role of the knower to the structures of the pre-existing object. Essentially, the knower is at the mercy of the to-be-known. If he succeeds in knowing, it is *not* because he came prewired to do so (innatism), but because he saw, heard, touched, tasted, or smelled the to-be-known object. Thus empiricism, in the strict behavioral sense, assumes that what we know has been inscribed upon us by the environment. Intellectually, we are products of the experiences which we have had with our environment, that "all cognitive information has its source in objects so that the subject is instructed by what is outside him (Piaget, 1972b, p. 19)."

A great many contemporary theorists subscribe to this epistemology, foremost among them is, of course, B.F. Skinner. For these theorists, learning (or more generally, direct experience) has occupied a central role in psychology. This is not an accident, it is a calculated search based on an epistemological foundation. B.F. Skinner (e.g., 1953) has written extensively about the role of the environment in changing people's behavior. In his *Science and Human Behavior,* Skinner (1953) cautioned against any type of innatist position in explaining human behavior. In improving the scientific stature of psychology, Skinner (1953) warned:

> The practice of looking inside the organism for an explanation of behavior has tended to obscure the variables which are immediately available for a scientific analysis. *These variables lie outside the organism,* in its immediate environmental history. They have a physical status to which the usual techniques of science are adapted, and they make it possible to explain behavior as other subjects are explained in science. These *independent variables* are of many sorts and their relations to behavior are often subtle and complex, but we cannot hope to give an adequate account of behavior without analyzing them (p. 31).

Skinner goes on to say that the science of human behavior must be built on the relationships between independent variables which lie outside the organism and the dependent variables or the resultant behavior (p. 35).

In this vein, Skinner (1953) continues to "explain" in a cause-effect way such human phenomena as thinking, government, religion, psychotherapy, economic control and education. His endeavor culminates with the question of human culture and the design of such cultures. In short, Skinner maintains that environmental contingencies shape behavior, and the science of psychology should be devoted to explicating the effects of environmental events upon behavior. Inner states should be avoided in such an endeavor for "they are not relevant in a functional analysis (p. 35)." Thus, knowledge structures do not have their roots in innate programming. Indeed, according to this view knowledge is possible only through information that is available outside the subject.

CONSTRUCTIVISM

A third position of which Piaget is the major current advocate, is termed *constructivist*. According to Piaget, knowledge formation is neither preformed nor is it a direct reflection of our experiences. Knowledge formation occurs as a result of the subject's actions upon the object. Abstractions are formed from this interaction, and these abstractions are in fact constructed by the subject. Through his actions upon the object, the subject comes to discover what to him are its properties. Viewed from the psychogenetic perspective, discovery is not a passive process but a construction of the knower, since what is discovered is always a function of what is already known. What is more is that through his activity the subject also abstracts properties of his own actions. In this way, knowledge grows in the subject: by constructing mental structures (organizations) of reality, by working on reality. To repeat, Piaget contents that the formation of mental structures are in fact personal constructions, not mere copies of reality. In short, to know an object is to have acted upon that object.

Perhaps the most fundamental principle of Piagetian epistemology is that knowledge is equated with activity. Piaget (1972a, p. 78) states that:

> . . . to know an object is to act upon it and to transform it . . . To know is therefore to assimilate reality into structures of transformation, and these are the structures that intelligence constructs as a direct extension of our actions.

In a word, intelligence is action, and action transforms the schemes of other actions. To paraphrase Piaget (1972a, p. 29) to know is to be able to execute and coordinate actions. Initially such actions are on a physical level, yet soon they are internalized and are conceptually represented. In fact as the individual develops intellectually he comes to rely less and less on the physical aspects of intellectual activity and more and more on the internalization of this activity.

All of this leads to the epistemologically significant point that knowing is not a picture-taking process; it does not consist of copying the external world. Indeed, quite the converse is true: knowledge is a process of mental activity that reconstructs the external world. The schemes underlying our potential activity determine, in larg measure, what is perceived and how it is comprehended. In this sense, a case can easily be made that what is known—both in terms of content and mental process—determines what is perceived. With Smith (1975), it can be argued that comprehension determines perception. This principle is pivotal to the understanding of genetic cognitive psychology. Moreover, it completely contradicts the empiricist (behavioral) contention that out of perception arises comprehension. A number of studies can be cited that lead to this conclusion. A single yet dramatic illustration of this point is the fact that young children insist that the level of water in a glass will tilt with the glass (when the glass is tilted) despite the fact that they see that the water level remains parallel to the table top!

This principle has broad and significant implications for the educator. Since the subject's comprehension determines what he can perceive, and therefore learn, the educator must understand and deal with differing levels (stages) of cognitive development. Once again this calls for educators to be students of developmental cognitive psychology; to recognize the real attainments and limitations that define each stage of intellectual growth: The educator cannot expect students to react to material in the same way regardless of how precisely the material may be presented. Students react actively to educational materials in the sense that they attempt to make sense of the material by relating it to *what* they already know. More importantly, they relate to the material in terms of *how* they can think.

The Diachronic Nature of Knowledge Formation

The active nature of knowledge formation of which Piaget speaks clearly places the burden of this formation on the subject. But the subject does not stand still in time. His cognitive structures are not *synchronic*, they do not remain static over time. For Piaget (e.g.,

1972b) knowledge formation obeys general laws set by time. How a subject apprehends a phenomenon changes with the developmental stage of that subject. Thus, a fundamental aspect of knowledge is that it is time-dependent or *diachronic*. More specifically, Piaget's genetic psychology has shown us that, over the course of one's development, knowledge formation is a nonlinear process, with qualitatively different types of thinking characterizing each stage of the process. These stages are related to age but only in a broad sense, for maturation is but one of several factors that contribute to intellectual development. Thus, unlike innatists who focus on maturation—or the development of the nervous system over time—as an explanation for the unfolding of preformed knowledge structures, Piaget contends that maturation is necessary but not sufficient in explaining the evolution of knowledge. As we shall see, the factors of physical experience, social transmission, and internal self-regulation all must interact in the development of intellectual structures over time. Piaget's analysis of the diachronic, or time-dependent, changes that characterize the human intellect has resulted in his well known concept of intellectual stage. The stage component of the theory highlights the various levels of structuring that take place in the course of human intellectual development. For Piaget, intelligence, or, more precisely, the construction of reality over time, is a nonlinear phenomenon. Intelligence, Piaget argues, is constructed by the subject in a successive, spiral-like fashion, each spiral constituting a qualitatively different (superior) form on construction than the preceding one. Piaget has described four major stages in this process of mental development. Since these stages have been repeatedly and extensively treated by Piaget himself as well as numerous others, only a brief sketch of these stages will be outlined below.

SENSORIMOTOR INTELLIGENCE (BIRTH TO 18-24 MONTHS)

Generally speaking, the sensorimotor period is characterized by the infant's continuous exploration of the surrounding environment through his immediate senses. Exploration of the environment by the infant is at first accomplished through hereditary structures (reflexes and primitive perceptions). Mental organization is at first limited to these inborn reflexes as well as to perceptions, e.g., perception of form and depth. In other words, the infant tries to organize knowledge and adapt to the world by relying fundamentally on elaborations of the reflexes and other hereditary structures with which he is born. Infants adapt to the world by touching, sucking, pulling, pushing objects, etc. Objects are known to the extent that the child can directly and physically act upon them. At first the infant is so ego-centric or self-centered that he is unaware of anything else but himself. He is even unaware of himself as separate from the world around him. He can make sense only of objects that he is capable of touching, seeing, smelling, tasting, and hearing. And because he cannot relate these sensory and perceptual stimuli to any previous knowledge, these experiences are at first isolated from one another. By coordinating and elaborating upon these sensorimotoric forms of intelligence, the infant learns to adapt to his surroundings in a more flexible way. He quickly learns to turn his head in the direction of a noise-making object, to reach and grasp objects, to follow a moving object with his eyes, etc. He begins to *differentiate* these acts from one another and from himself as the carrier of these acts as well as to integrate them so as to attain new goals. In this way his behavior grows more intentional, more adaptable, i.e., more intelligent. By the end of this period the child has built up, in a rudimentary fashion, all the structures of thought that he will need. He has shown an intrinsic curiosity in the world around him to observe, explore, discover, invent and test.

STAGE 1: (0-1 MONTH)

Before the age of one month the neonate is restricted to exercising his reflexes. Piaget (1967) regards these reflexes as the neonate's first schemata (or plans) for adapting.* This knowledge system is restricted to such ways of knowing as grasping, sucking, crying, eye-movements, etc. The Stage 1 child adapts through assimilation of objects into these sensorimotor schemata. If the object cannot be changed to fit the child's inherent sensorimotor schemata, it simply does not get known. However, some advances are made during the first month of life in *refining* these reflexes. For example, the sucking reflex becomes more and more refined in the sense that it becomes more efficient in locating the nipple.

STAGE 2: (1-4 MONTHS)

At about the age of one month the separate schemata such as sucking, grasping, vocalizing, etc., being to be "integrated into habits and organized percepts (Piaget, 1967, p. 10)." Coordination of these schemata—the major attainment of the Stage 2 child—takes place due to the newly developed possibility for small accomodations. Now the child can change himself by coordinating separate schemata to meet the demands of the situation, as when the child turns his head to orient in the direction of a sound. Hand-eye coordination, another instance of schema coordination, enables the child to grasp an object (toy) and put it in her mouth. Piaget (1967) points out that this development signals the beginning of the possibility for changing a schema as a result of interacting with the world. In effect, now the child can acquire habits. It may be said that the rudiments of "play" and "imitation" begin to manifest themselves. Here play is, however, limited to reproducing a behavior which the child has produced by chance. Piaget (1952) labeled these repetitive actions *primary circular reactions*. These reactions are actions that are initially produced without intention but, once created, can be repeated. However, Piaget is careful to point out that these reactions are not merely mechanically repeated; rather as they are repeated they incorporate (assimilate) new objects onto themselves. Once a schema has been developed, whether intentionally or not, it must function. In terms of cognitive motivation, one can say that schemata, especially those that are not well established or equilibrated, *want* to function! Also, once a schema has been developed it will tend to generalize to other objects, incorporating other objects onto itself.

STAGE 3: (4-8 MONTHS)

Piaget refers to the third stage (4-8 months) of sensorimotor intelligence as the stage of *secondary circular reactions,* meaning that the child has a tendency to repeat a motoric act of her own that results, quite by chance, in an interesting environmental outcome. The infant will then repeat this activity over and over again. For example, by thrashing his legs about in his crib a baby notices the mobile suspended above is moving. She will then repeat this action to produce movements in the mobile. The significant feature here is that this act is not intentional in the sense that the goal (moving the mobile) was conceived prior to the means which brought it about (thrashing her legs). Rather, the act is said to be semi-intentional in that the child thinks of the goal *after* he has already put the action in motion. That is, unlike the habitual modes of responding characteristic of the Stage 2 infant, the Stage 3 infant is beginning to be aware of physical causality. However, even though secondary circular reactions are semi-intentional, they are unlike primary circular reactions in that they involve the outside world, not just the infant's own body.

STAGE 4 (8-12 MONTHS)

The ability to use various means to attain a goal first appears at around 8 months. Here there are clear indications that the infant is capable of true intentional action in an effort to achieving a goal. Intentionality is inferred from a number of behaviors that Piaget has illustrated. For example, in one of his observations Piaget (1952, p.

219) shows his son, Laurent, an object but places his hand in front of it as an obstacle but with the object still in view of the child. Piaget notes that at 7 months, 17 days Laurent tries to get the object by hitting the obstacle, while at 9 months, 15 days, Laurent pushes the obstacle with one hand while grabbing the object with the other. It is clear from this observation that Laurent's action is intentional in that it shows separation of the means from the ends. This is, in order to attain his goal, Laurent had to push his father's hand away. Moreover, the infant's actions demonstrate that he has invented a *new coordination* between his various schemata. It is the ability to intend to attain a goal, independent of the means that the infant will employ, and the invention of new coordinations that is the hallmarks of the Stage 4 child.

STAGE 5 (12-18 MONTHS)

Piaget (1952) has labelled the fifth stage of sensorimotor intelligence the stage of *tertiary circular reactions,* because the repetitive acts of the Stage 5 child are neither "primary" in the sense they are exercises unintentionally initiated by the body, nor "secondary" in that they are directed toward the environment to make "an interesting spectacle last." Tertiary actions are repetitive behaviors with an experimental bent. The child acts to discover ways in which he can manipulate an object. The separation of means from ends in now clearly established. Gone are the days of repeating an act to simply reproduce a result. Now the child varies his movements as if to observe how the variations in his actions will differ in the outcomes that they produce. In short, tertiary circular reactions may be said to constitute the beginning of the know-how of experimentation. The goal is to discover *new* properties of objects and events. This essentially accommodatory tendency leads the child to use new means to achieve the same end. He discovers that he can pull objects toward him by pulling a string or tilt them to get them through the bars of his playpen. In other words, his trial and error behavior is directed toward a goal. Piaget labels this behavior "direct groping" since the experimentation is carried out physically not mentally, e.g., the child does not think out the solution of how to get the object through the bars of the playpen, but in fact tries it one way and then another until he succeeds. Piaget (1952) focused on the child's ability to pull objects to themselves. He noticed that in this stage the child could use one object as an intermediary to obtain another object. For instance, a toy resting on a blanket could be drawn near by pulling the blanket closer. This activity requires differentation and re-coordination of already existing schemata. But the application of the new schemata coordination is not reflected upon, it is carried out physically in groping to discover new means to an end.

STAGE 6 (18-24 MONTHS)

In the sixth and last stage of sensorimotor intelligence, the child begins to do his groping mentally rather than physically. As Piaget puts it, the child's physical or motor action is "interiorized", i.e., the child thinks about how he would do something without actually doing it, until she mentally reaches a satisfactory solution. Piaget calls this "the invention of new means through mental combinations." By contrast, the Stage 5 intelligence was characterized not by *invention* of new means but by "discovery of new means through active experimentation." The child at this last stage is making the transition from physical to mental actions (thought, and she can represent action in a semiotic way without actually performing it. In short, the Stage 6 child can symbolically *represent* his actions upon an object, he can mentally *invent* new means to an end, and these acts imply an advanced form of intentional, goal-directed action. Piaget infers that this type of mental coordination is taking place because here the child, when confronted with a problem, shows little or no direct groping followed by a sudden action. This *insight* into the new problem is indicative of mental groping.

The six stages mentioned above constitutes a very brief summary of the development of sensorimotr intelligence, or the logic that characterizes sensorimotoric actions. It is evident that acts of intelligence do not evolve in a vacuum, they require interactions with objects of knowledge., with content. It is through this interaction that the infant construct his knowledge of reality. Thus, following *The Origins of Intelligence in Children* (1952) originally published in French in 1936—Piaget (1954) published *The Construction of Reality in the Child*. As the title indicates, it is the latter book that relates the growth of sensorimotor intelligence to the specific categories of knowledge which Kant had initially formulated, namely, the permanent object, space, time, and casuality. In *The Construction of Reality in the Child,* Piaget showed how the infant constructs his practical knowledge of these categories of knowledge through his sensorimotor intelligence.

PREOPERATIONAL THOUGHT (2 TO 7 YEARS)

The formation of the *symbolic function* signals the end of sensorimotor intelligence and the beginning of preoperational thought.**

The symbolic function enables the child to represent objects that are not in his immediate environment. In other words, the symbolic function enables the child to let one thing stand for something else. This very important function is manifested through *words*, through *symbolic play*, as well as through *mental symbols*. The mental symbol, which does not involve languages, may be an image (visual or auditory) or it may take the form of "abbreviated movement." Whatever its form, Piaget believes that the mental symbol has its origin in imitation. Symbolic play occupies much of the child's time. Here, the child plays all sorts of "pretend" games. Finally language takes on an important role in that it allows the child to convey ideas and feelings to others.† Piaget (1950) divides this stage into the preconceptual stage and the intuitive stage.

PRECONCEPTUAL THOUGHT (1½ YEARS TO 4 YEARS)

The preconceptual child is investigative. He asks "how" and "why" questions and normally does not lack "explanations" to such questions. His "explanations" are preconceptual in that he can think but not about his own thinking. As a result, his thinking is *egocentric* (seeing situations from his own point of view and no one else's), *animistic* (attributing life to non-living things), *artificialistic* (ascribing causes to non-physical agents such as Gods), and *participatory* (believing that he causes phenomenon of nature to occur). This phenomenon manifests itself vividly in the child's attempt to understand *relations* among objects of knowledge, such as cause-effect relations. A preconceptual child trips over a rock and blames the rock for his fall.

INTUITIVE THOUGHT (4 TO 7-8 YEARS)

Together, preconceptual thought and intuitive thought make up preoperational intelligence. Thus, intuitive thought is a continuation and an extension of preconceptual thought. Intuitive thought is also characterized by *egocentricity*. Additionally, the child has explanations for all events, except that these explanations are still quite personal and not tied down to any external or objective system of description or explanation. For example, to a five year-old a care is alive because it runs! The child of intuitive thought offers explanations that are perfectly intuitively reasonable to *him*, yet the explanations may be contradictory when viewed from without. For example, children will use their body to measure the length of an object. If the experimenter gives them a stick with which to measure two towers to see if they are the same height, they may use the stick in a horizontal way—as a level—to determine equivalence of the two towers. When given a considerably shorter stick children resort to some intuitive method, holding the shorter stick vertically against the tower and telling the experimenter to see that "so much" was left at the top when held next to one tower, and about the same is left when held next to the second tower. The act of repeating the measurement operation several times does not occur to them. This is critical for it shows that these children are still incapable of conceptualizing transformations or changes over time or space. That is, they tend to base their thinking on end states, or how the object ends up after a transformation has been performed on it. Furthermore, preoperational children do not show any sign of thinking through the use of quantitative concepts. Their logic is preoperational, meaning it is not yet capable of performing a series of actions on the object and keeping track of such actions. Thus, in effect, preoperational children are pre-transformational; they tend to center on the results (end states) as opposed to the processes by which the results were obtained (transformations), because they are more or less bound to their perception.

As is evident from what was said thus far, intellectual growth begins in motor actions (in the sensorimotor stage) and moves to a level in which actions have been interiorized viz. a viz. the semiotic (symbolic) function (in the preoperational stage). The third level of intellectual development, called operational, is qualitatively different from its predecessors in that it is characterized by the ability to carry out transformations upon objects of knowledge without destroying the invariant properties of such objects. The term "operation" in Piaget's theory refers to organized action groupings that show identity, closure, associativity, and most importantly reversibility. Thus, intellectual operations are indeed *actions,* actions that are characterized by (a) generality, (b) reversibility, (c) integrity, and (d) universality. Operations are general in that they apply not only to isolated cases but to all aspects of a particular action. For example, adding applies not only to adding oranges and oranges but also to adding oranges and lemons. Operations are reversible for they enable thought to retrace its steps, keeping track of such retracing. For example, the operational child understands that a ball of clay will remain the same in weight despite changes performed on its shape. Notice that this reversible transformation has not destroyed the conceptual invariance, i.e., the amount of clay will remain invariant even when we perform such reversible transformations upon it. This grouping of actions constitute a *system,* an integrated whole, not isolated actions. For example, one cannot operationally know a number (say, the number 10) unless it is tied in with other numbers in a systematic way. Finally, as Piaget and Inhelder (1969) point out, intellectual operations apply not only to one individual, but to all those who are on the same intellectual plane. Thus, operations exist universally within a particular group of individuals. The term "preoperational" stems from the fact that the structures of thought of this stage have not yet developed into action that manifest the above mentioned characteristics.

Piaget and Inhelder (1969) go on to describe reasons for the delay of operational thought in children. Why doesn't operational thought emerge sooner than the ages of 7 or 8 years? The answer, according to these authors, lies in several obstacles that the preoperational child must overcome. One of these obstacles is the lag which exists between well developed motoric acts and their mental representation. An example of this lag is given by Piaget and Inhelder (1969, pp. 93-94).

> Children of four and five often go by themselves from home to school and back every day even though the walk may be ten minutes or so in length. Yet if you ask them to represent their path by means of little three-dimensional cardboard objects (houses, church, streets, river, squares, etc.) or to indicate the plan of the school as it is seen from the main entrance or from the side facing the river, they are unable to reconstruct the topographical relationship, even though they constantly utilize them in action.

A second obstacle lies in the tendency for preschool children to "center" on certain physical features of a situation, ignoring other salient ones. The process of decentering, the progressive process of viewing an object from other perspectives, does consume much time and it is not until the seventh year of life that it finally is attained. A third obstacle to operational thought is related to the second in that others also have opinions now that they can represent symbolically. Reconciling these opinions with one's own is the third obstacle. In short, operational thought requries decenteration. Overcoming these obstacles is no small task and it takes the better of five years (after the sensorimotor period) to attain.

CONCRETE OPERATIONAL THOUGHT (7 YEARS TO ABOUT 12 YEARS)

Among the newly developed structures in this operational period are the abilities to conserve, seriate, and classify, on the basis of quantity. It should be noted, however, that this period of operational thought is in reality divisible into the stage of *concrete* operational thought (7 to 12 years) as distinguished from the stage *formal* operational thought (12 or so and over). Essentially, the distinction focuses on whether the child can perform mental operations on concrete objects only (concrete operations) or whether the child can carry out such operations hypothetically (formal operations).

By the age of 7 or 8 most normal children have reached a period where the series of actions that they can perform on objects of knowledge are in fact organized and have been interiorized. Operational thought is transformational thought. The child can think about his own thinking. He is capable of performing transformations, and in fact reversing them if necessary. For example, the operational child understands that a ball of clay will remain the same in *amount* despite changes performed on its shape. Recall that the preoperational child is incapable of thinking even in the most elementary mathematical terms, i.e., he cannot understand the fact that if $4 + 4 = 8$, then $8 - 4 = 4$. On the other hand, the concrete operational child is indeed capable of using quantitative concepts in his thinking. *Amount* is a quantitative concept. Thus, not only can the concrete operational child think in terms of quantities, but he can perform transformations on his quantitative concepts (e.g., reversing a transformation to arrive at the starting position). Yet the concrete operational child has a limitation: he cannot exercise his mental operations in a completely hypothetical or abstract situation. His operational logic is bound to the real. His basis for thinking is reality, and from it he can extend it to the realm of possibility. Strategies involved in playing chess are not possible for this child; basing a series of thoughts on probability is difficult; reasoning involving the systematic testing of all possible combinations of a set of items is not possible. In short, the child is a logical thinker, but only when he can begin with the real. These limitations can prevent the child from conducting experiments because they are not yet able to think of the possible variables that can cause the effect, manipulating one variable at a time while holding all others constant. In short, reality dominates possibility for this child.

FORMAL OPERATIONAL THOUGHT (11-12 YEARS AND OVER)

Preadolescence and adolescence is marked by a number of developmental events which transform the child into an adult physically, emotionally, socially and, as we shall see, intellectually. By the age of 12 or so, the intellectual limitations associated with the concrete operational child seem to gradually disappear. The adolescent, at least in urbanized and industrialized societies, begins to function intellectually in ways that are quite distinguishable from the elementary school child of similar cultural background. Unlike the concrete operational child, the formal thinker shows flexibility in thought. He can think in abstract terms, in hypothetical terms and in deductive terms. He can think of a number of possibilities in a given situation simultaneously. He can think in terms of proportions, correlations, and probability. All of these competencies are said to be operative in formal thinkers. Depending on the familiarity with a content area, the theory predicts that adults, more or less universally, will utilize such concepts in their thinking. In the next chapter we shall explore the validity of this prediction. For now, let us be content with understanding the theory as well as the results of experimentation stemming from the theory.

In short, the period of formal thought constitutes a new level of equilibrium in the structures of thought, one which is substantially different (higher) from the equilibrium which characterized the concrete operational period. The reader may now ask: What is it about the action of the adolescent that warrants our speaking of a new equilibrium, a new form of thought? This question can best be answered in terms of: (a) the functions that adolescents *can* perform that were previously not intheir repertoire, and (b) the structures whose presence must be inferred to be operative given that adolescents function in new ways. An obvious method for exploring these questions is to analyze the thinking processes of children and adolescents as they attempt to solve certain tasks, tasks which are specifically designed to tease apart the thought processos the two sets of subjects. Such tasks have been worked out in great detail by Inhelder and Piaget (1958) in *The Growth of Logical Thinking from Childhood to Adolescense,* which is truly a landmark in this area.

Everything that was said about concrete operations applies to formal operations. In addition, the stage of formal operations implies the ability to use mental operations (e.g., reversing a transformation) hypothetically while keeping track of the consequence. Aside from being capable of hypothetical reasoning, the formal operational individual can: (1) formulate hypotheses in a scientific sense and test them out, which involves separation and control of variables; (2) think in terms of proportions, as opposed to mere differences; and (3) use combinatorial analyses, which involve keeping track of various combinations of variables. Thus, a number of attainments characterize the formal operational child. The most general characteristics, however, is the child's newly developed ability to subordinate *reality* to *possibility.* Whereas concrete operational thought moves from what it considers to be real (concretely present) to an extension of this reality in terms of what is *potentially* likely, formal thought can begin with possibility and then reduce reality to an instance of that which is possible. It is this subordination of reality to possibility that enables thought to deal with a series of combinations simultaneously. In short, formal operations enable the individual to comprehend abstract concepts in a logically coherent and empirically sound way.

General Implications

By way of educational implications, Piaget's description of the course of intellectual development, which has been repeatedly verified (with minor exceptions), has a great deal to add to the older version of active education. Active educational methods now must consider the stages of mental development which characterize students. The child can no longer be viewed as a miniaturized adult who has the same mental equipment as the adult but who lacks information that the adult already possesses. Nor can we assume that all adults are capable of formal operations. Moreover, we cannot assume that the "child is a little flower; given time and nourishment, it will grow." Here the learner is viewed as a constructor of knowledge, as an active agent in the formation of his own knowledge. But his active construction of knowledge is not only dependent upon the availability and quality of physical experience and social stimulation, it is also dependent on maturation. Educationally speaking, there is one danger in drawing implications for education from Piaget's description of stages of intellectual development: that danger is to consider them immutably fixed, beginning at one point in time and ending in another. (Piaget's main concern has always been with the succession of the various stages, not with when they occur exactly. In this respect, Piaget has always exercised a great deal of caution, mentioning ages as rough and approximate time periods in the epistemic subject, not in every real subject. Thus, the task is not merely one of finding a strict isomorphism between age and curriculum, a strict *match,* but a secondary isomorphism, one which adapts the curriculum to the psycho-epistemic characteristics of the individual student). On the contrary, cognitive development is a product of interaction of all factors mentioned above. Thus, the theory upon which constructive methods rest "believes in the possibility of influencing that development (Piaget, 1972a, p. 170)."

It should, however, be pointed out that "influencing" development is substantially different from "accelerating" development. By now, the so-called "American question" of whether and how to accelerate intellectual development is well known. In answer to this question, Piaget has systematically taken the position that acceleration of intellectual development is undesirable, and educators would do well not to engage in it. If educators should not accelerate the rate of development from one stage to the next, what then is their role in educating? Doesn't "influencing" imply "accelerating"? Is there a potential contradiction in what Piaget has said? To me, no contradiction exists. First, acceleration carries with it a conscious and active effort on the part of an educational agent (e.g., a teacher, a curriculum specialist) to deliberately speed up the rate of acquisition of the very mental operations which define a given stage of development. Since maturation is a factor in the development of intellectual development, and educators can do nothing to speed up this factor, acceleration procedures necessarily will be limited. Secondly, these mental operations are only illustrative of the kind of thinking of which students in certain stages are capable. To reduce education to these mental operations is not what constructivistic education is all about. The main role of a teacher in constructivistic education is to provide a physical and social environment which is most conducive to observation, exploration, manipulation, inquiry, discovery, invention, etc. in an effort to afford the learner opportunities to pursue his own knowledge-forming activity. Given adequate maturation, students will naturally form these mental operations, but their education would not have been limited to these mental operations.‡ Thus, the question of education is much broader than that of acceleration, the former being viewed in terms of the conditions which will stimulate self-initiated activity on the part of the student, the latter being restricted to training on specific Piagetian tasks. To emphasize, without appropriate structures students cannot be expected to learn. This is so no matter how much repetition and drill is provided. To make a point, an ordinary ten-year-old cannot be expected to grasp concepts of (simple) relativity. This conclusion is based on the contention that knowledge acquisition is an interactive process, requring a match between subject and the object of knowledge. In this case, the match does not exist, and no amount of practice or drill will result in the subject's comprehension of this phenomenon.

This genetic point of view clashes rather sharply with the behavioral point of view which has elevated the role of the environment to unwarranted importance. The unfortunate aspect of the behavioral emphasis on external, environmental stimuli in the learning process is that it creates the fallacious assumption among educators that "if only we could arrange our presentation in such a way, our students will learn such and such . . . " Constructivistic principles do not lead to this problem, for they do not assume that the magic of learning is in the teacher, the design of the curriculum materials, or any other agent that lies outside the learner. Rather, the magic of learning and knowing lies in the interaction between the subject and the object of knowledge.

Knowledge formation is an interactive process, requiring appropriate interchange between the subject and the object of knowledge. What can be learned from such interaction depends in large measure on the stage of intellectual development of the learner.

---

*A schema (singular for schemata) is an organized aspect of intelligence, a plan for action.

*For Piaget, reflex is not an unconditioned response that is conditioned through experience. Rather, a reflex is a reaction that is hereditary and one that is capable of further adaptation. In other words, a reflex is not a mechanical response. It is a reaction capable of self-regulation. For instance, with experience, the sucking reaction becomes more specialized, more efficient, etc.

**Piaget uses the term "intelligence" to refer to sensorimotor adaptations while he reserves the term "thought" to refer to all periods which follow. This is not accidental for sensorimotor intelligence is not in any way reflective.

†We shall treat the problem of the importance of language, as a symbolic activity, in the process of education in a later section.

‡It has been shown that unschooled children attain various mental operations even though they lag behind schooled children (e.g., Goodnow & Bethon, 1966).

4 Factors in the Growth of Knowledge

Now that we have sketched an outline of how knowledge is formed, it would be instructive to ask what the factors are that determine the development of that knowledge. Obviously, if we could identify these factors, then it would help us explain the development of knowledge. And if we could identify these factors, we might be able to influence them so that we could enhance the development of knowledge. So, what are these factors? How do these factors make knowledge development possible? How can these factors be influenced in an effort to help the process of knowledge formation?

Factors In Knowledge Development

As a developmental constructivist, Piaget (1970) maintains that intellectual development comes about through a continuous interaction between environmental factors and hereditary structures. Specifically, he believes that the four factors of maturation, social transmission, physical experience, and equilibration are all necessary, and indeed sufficient, in explaining intellectual development (Piaget, 1961).

MATURATION

Piaget (1961) defines *maturation* in terms of the gradual differentiation of biological systems. Heredity equips us all with certain biological structures that mature and decay with age. Biological structures, particularly the central nervous system, must mature in order that cognitive development can take place. No one would deny the indispensible role which the maturation of these physical structures plays in the development of cognitive structures. However, as necessary as maturation is, it is not sufficient.

If we were to explain the development of intelligence solely on the basis of maturation we would expect to find no substantial differences in the pattern and rate of development across all human cultures. Yet, we know from cross-cultural research studies (e.g., Berry and Dasen, 1973) that while the pattern is constant, the rate differs from culture to culture. That is, while the sequence of appearance of the stages of intellectual development do not vary from culture to culture, some cultures—and some subgroups within certain cultures—tend to lag behind in attaining these stages (more specific results will be discussed later in this chapter). Thus, the idea that knowledge is preformed by heredity and it simply unfolds as a function of time is not acceptable. Within the framework of developmental constructivism, it is assumed that the subject must interact with a physical and social world in order for it to develop. These cultural delays indicate that there is more to intellectual development than just being equipped with the neurophysiological structures that differentiate with time. In order to adapt, every biological structure must function in some ecologically valid environment. Intellectual development is seen as an extension of this sort of adaptation, an extension into psychological adaptation.

PHYSICAL EXPERIENCE

Physical experience, the second necessary condition in the development of knowledge, is defined in terms of the interchange that the child has with the physical environment around him. Piaget (1961) argues that physical experience consists of acting on objects. In acting upon objects of knowledge, two types of knowledge are abstracted. On the one hand, physical experience results in knowledge (abstractions) about the properties of the objects themselves. For example, a child may observe that a cylinder rolls when he pushes it, that a mobile turns when he hits it, that objects fall down when he drops them, and that a rock feels heavier than a feather. In this sense physical experience results in *simple abstraction,* or in integration of all these simple abstractions into a coherent system resulting in what is termed *empirical knowledge.* On the other hand, as knowers act upon objects of knowledge, they come to realize that they can exercise control over their own actions. In this sense, actions are being taken upon actions, i.e., co-ordination of actions. This results in knowledge about the ways in which actions can manipulate other actions. When this occurs on a symbolic level, we have thinking about one's own thinking, or the beginning of inferential thinking. Piaget gives the following example. A child who realizes that ten pebbles will remain ten regardless of whether he arranges them in a row or a circle has abstracted knowledge not about the physical properties of the pebbles themselves but about the actions (both physical and mental) that he has taken on those pebbles. A child who understands that ten pebbles can be evenly divided among four of his friends and himself has done the same thing. When physical experience results in abstractions (knowledge) about the properties of the actions themselves, we have what is referred to as *reflective abstraction.* The integration of all of these reflective abstractions result in what Piaget has called *logico-mathmatical knowledge.*

These two types of abstraction—simple vs. reflective—are not the same, nor is the difference between them a trivial one. Whereas simple abstraction refers to *discovery* of the physical properties of objects, reflective abstraction refers to *inventions* about the properties of one's own physical as well as mental actions. Thus, from the same physical experience, two different types of knowledge emerge: empirical knowledge and logico-mathematical knowledge. As one can readily see, physical experience, in the sense of acting on and interacting with objects of knowledge, is absolutely vital to the growth of knowledge; knowledge not only about the properties of objects, but also of thinking itself.* Vital as this factor is in the growth of knowledge, it is still not sufficient to explain that growth. We must consider the social context in which the knower is brought up as well.

SOCIAL TRANSMISSION

A third factor influencing the development of knowledge is *social transmission*. This factor refers to experience with people and people-invented schemes. Unlike animals, people have developed cultures. They have invented methods for creating, accumulating, and transmitting artifacts, values, and knowledge. The young are therefore not raised in a social vacuum. They are raised in a cultural context. Through specific channels of this context, most notably art, language, and education, children gain enormous amounts of socially inherited knowledge. Social transmission refers to knowledge that results from interaction of the child with other people in a cultural context.

To grasp the significance of the factor of social transmission and its impact upon intellectual development, one need only turn to illustrations of cross-cultural research in Piagetian psychology. As Dasen (1977) points out, the primary purpose of this type of research is to test the universality of Piaget's theory of the development of intellectual processes and to examine the degree to which cultural factors determine these processes. Suffice it to say that the overwhelming evidence tends to support Piaget's claim of the universal *sequence* of stages and substages. But more germane to the present discussion is the ubiquitous finding that the closer a culture is to an educated, urbanized, and industrialized culture, the faster the *rate* of intellectual development of children from that culture. Thus, while the elements of schooling, urbanization, industrialization seem to influence the *rate* of development, the nature of development itself is not susceptible to cultural variations. Apparently, the attainments of the concepts as well as their sequence is culturally invariant.

A second line of investigation also supports the contention that children's intellectual evolution through the steps and substages described by Piaget is influenced by cultural factors. For example, Scribner (1976, p. 17) observe that "within each culture there is a large discrepancy in performance between schooled and non-schooled. With schooling, there is little between culture variation in performance for the cultures studied." In sum, according to a variety of recent literature, it appears that although there may be delays in intellectual development, the sequence and eventual attainment of these stages are universal. This is not to say that all people within all cultures attain the highest levels of reasoning. Quite the contrary, remote cultures do not seem to manifest the higher levels of development. And research in America indicates that approximately fifty percent of the high school graduates do not spontaneously use formal operational reasoning. Obviously, this type of research is very difficult to conduct and to interpret for a number of reasons, and it is for this reason that value-judgements should not be made with respect to a given culture's inferiority, etc. The obvious reasons include: (a) the choice of the concepts chosen for study, and (b) the cultural background of the researcher (Piaget, 1971). Nonetheless, we can see that if the criterion of intellectual development is Piaget's theory, then schooling, urbanization, and industrialization are clearly elements of social transmission that must be considered.

Again, it must be pointed out that social transmission cannot account for intellectual development by itself. In addition to the factors of maturation, physical experience, and social transmission Piaget has described a fourth factor which he considers to be—in many senses— the backbone of intellectual growth. Piaget has called this fourth and crucial factor "equilibration".

EQUILIBRATION

To illustrate the role of *equilibration* in the intellectual growth patterns of children, I would like to pose the following question: What does it take for a plant to grow and achieve its potential? My students ordinarily answer by saying that a plant will need water, it will need sunshine, it will need nourishment, and so on. The factor that is usually left out is the seed and, more importantly, the mechanism that must be inherent in the seed to enable it to make use of the water, sunshine, and nourishment in a balanced way. In other words, the factor that is usually left out is the requirement that the plant must have an internal mechanism of self-regulation, the factor whose business it is to strike a balance among the various factors with which it interacts. As Furth** pointed out, if a toothpick is stuck in rich soil, given sufficient amount of nutrition, sunshine, etc., it would rot! In short, equilibration refers to the intrinsic process of effecting a balance (a momentary equilibrium) between the factors of maturation, physical experience, and social transmission, a balance between what is already known and what the knower is attempting to comprehend.

While this is a difficult concept to grasp, it is central to Piaget's theory. It would therefore be useful to elaborate on this concept a bit. Recently, Furth (1977) and Piaget (1978) have offered some clarification of this rather slippery concept. Based on Piaget's theorizing, several points can be made: First, equilibration is a dynamic process intrinsic to cognitive life. Second, it is a process that contains its own feedback mechanism, thereby making it possible for an action to correct itself in the sense of searching for and reaching a more coherent form of equilibrium. For Piaget, this auto-regulatory mechanism is the fundamental motivational factor behind intellectual growth. Its major function is to search for more adaptive forms of equilibrium in the structures of thought. This is necessary in so far as further physical experiences or social transmissions tend to upset existing structures of thought. Equilibration is the process through which restoration of balance is achieved on a higher level, and it is achieved through the person's own activity. In this way, equilibration enables individuals to move from one state of balance (one stage of cognitive development) to a slightly higher one. Inhelder (1971, p. 33) states: "Piaget showed that cognitive development has a direction, and proceeds towards better and better adaptation of the knowing subject to the reality that is the object of knowledge." The point is that maturation, physical experience, and social transmission are necessary but not sufficient in explaining the movement in the direction of more internally consistent and adult-like thinking. Since cognitive structures are atemporal, it is necessary to explain how structures function in time, i.e., how they continually are readapted to function at higher and higher levels. In a phrase, the problem is to explain the dynamism that characterizes the development of cognitive structures which are themselves atemporal. In large part, the answer lies in the construct of equilibration.

On the level of cognition, equilibration is illustrated whenever an intellectual activity corrects itself as a result of its own outcome. That is, whenever an action receives feedback from its own results and adjusts itself accordingly we have an instance of equilibration. In solving a problem, we go through steps in our mind, and without the aid of any external information, decide that the steps might be in error. We rethink the steps and now the outcome clearly suggests that we are correct. This is an instance of the process of equilibration at work which results in a momentary state of equilibrium.

If one were to be confronted with logical absurdity he may or may not recognize the absurdity, depending upon his stage of intellectual development. If he does recognize it, then he is disequilibrated but quickly readjusts to equilibrium by dismissing the statement as fallacious. If, on the other hand, he does not even recognize the inherent absurdity, then he is not disequilibrated in the first place. For example, a child may state that a nail will sink in a tub of water because the nail is small. Then, when asked why a toothpick floats, he remarks that it is because it is small! To this child this logical contradiction is not one. A few months later he may be confused by that answer if we suggest that someone had made that remark. And a few months later he may state categorically that this explanation is not an adequate one. This example illustrates the process of equilibration, a continuous process of self-regulation, of finding a state of balance in thinking, of attempting to fit one concept with another and all the concepts into what one already knows.

The Development Of Knowledge

It should be observed that Piaget's theory of intelligence is strongly rooted in biological as well as logical foundations. We have seen, at least in one sense, that intelligence is linked with biology. Maturation is necessary to, and certainly defines the limits for, human functioning. We start with inherited and limited reflexes, and by integrating and differentiating and integrating and differentiating in other ways, we build more and more complex and flexible structures of knowledge. Throughout life we try to organize and reorganize our intellectual world in an effort to adapt on ever higher and higher planes. Thus, intellectual adaptation, is not static; it is dynamic, and with a direction. All this highlights the biological basis upon which the human intellect rests: biological adaptation extended to cognitive adaptation. In short, the business of intelligence is to seek more adaptive forms of organization. But a foundation does not constitute a building, for Piaget argues that intellectual structures are not *pre*formed; we must therefore try to find the means through which knowledge is constructed, i.e., we must find the mechanism through which this biological basis extends itself into the logical forms of adult human intelligence.

Figure 3 is a schematic representation of the four factors that are necessary and sufficient to intellectual growth as well as how these factors interact over time to develop higher forms of knowledge.

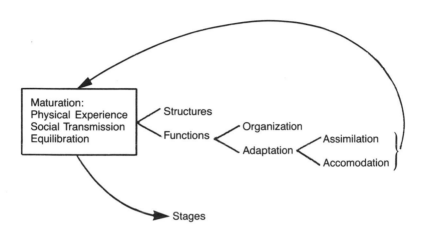

Fig. 3. Factors influencing the process of intellectual development.

Illustrated in Figure 3 is the interaction between maturation, physical experience, social transmission, and equilibration through intellectual functions and structures. *Structures* refers to organized aspects of intelligence, while *functions* consist of various modes of acting on the world. Intellectual structures are constructed of simpler organized aspects of knowledge. The simplest forms of these structural components of knowledge are the innate reflexes with which we are born. These reflexes are initially isolated from one another but soon they are integrated together to form more powerful organizations of knowledge. For example, a baby initially sucks, sneezes, orients with his eyes, shows startle responses, grasps objects that touch the palm of his hands, etc. Soon after birth, the baby learns to coordinate grasping with sucking, as when he is feeding. The new co-ordination (integration) represent a higher form of structure of his knowledge, enabling him to function in more adaptive ways. The baby soon adapts his grasping response to other objects; moreover, his sucking soon becomes more efficient and discriminating. In short, as he integrates his

47

structural aspects of knowledge, he also differentiates them. It is precisely this intrinsic ability to integrate and differentiate that is the secret of how structures of knowledge continue to grow in complexity as well as in flexibility. Eventually this integration and differention process creates logical structures that began as biological reflex actions. To appreciate how biological reflex actions get transformed into logical operations we need to look at how structures of knowledge are expressed, through functions. For example, infants learn to push, pull, follow objects visually, etc. With the aid of, and constant interaction among, these four factors in development the infant tends to coordinate isolated schemata into patterns consisting of two or more such schemata. With the advent of the symbolic system, which develops around the age of 18–24 months, these patterns become interiorized, i.e., represented mentally. In short, it is this representational system, consisting of mental images, words, etc., which enables physical actions to be translated into mental schemata. The continual integration and differentiation of physical actions and their mental counterparts results in more elaborate, organized, and flexible cognitive structures. As we have seen earlier, cognitive structures change, but the predisposition to function by organizing and adapting does not.

FUNCTIONAL INVARIANTS

Piaget (1952) postulates the existence of two functional invariants, i.e., modes of action, which do not change with maturation or experience. These two forms of functions are organization and adaptation. *Organization* refers to the tendency to integrate various experiences by integrating parts into wholes and wholes into more comprehensive wholes. The emphasis here is on the abstraction of relations and the relations between relations. As we interact with the world around us we tend to organize various parts of our experience into integrated wholes. This is true of perception, memory, language competence, and other intellectual activity. We are not passive with respect to our interaction with the world. We construct meaningful wholes from parts automatically. We may not be aware of this organizing activity, but we do it. For example, if you were asked to try to remember the following list— heaven, captain, kitchen, dinner, navy—you may construct a context which will include a captain of a navy ship in a kitchen eating dinner. A more primitive kind of organizing activity may be used to illustrate this functional invariant. In perception, size constancy is a familiar one, i.e., objects tend to look as big as they really are even when the distance between them and the observer increases greatly. That is, an adult will look as tall as an adult really is even when the retinal image of the adult (in the eyes of the observer) is considerably smaller as seen from a distance. Whether in perception, memory, or another cognitive activity, we tend to organize that with which we come in contact. As we organize we also adapt, that is, we tend to seek to adjust to our physical and intellectual world in increasingly more flexible ways. Thus, the second functional invariant is *adaptation*.

ASSIMILATION AND ACCOMMODATION

Piaget (1952) posits two adaptive processes: assimilation and accommodation. This is to say that adaptation—as a mode of coping with the world—takes two forms: assimilation and accommodation. *Assimilation* refers to the tendency to change that which we encounter to fit our existing structures of knowledge. That is, assimilation refers to the tendency for a person to act and think as he has acted and thought before. For example, if a child has learned to identify a dog correctly he will tend to identify similar animals (say sheep) as dogs. In this case the child is relating a new object of knowledge (sheep) to an old and organized aspect of his knowledge (dog). Relating new knowledge to already-existing structures is the form of adapting known as assimilation. Now if someone points out that the animal is not a dog, the child might have to change his habitual mode of acting and thinking and act and think as the situation demands. In this case, the child has to accommodate. He has to differentiate his old schema or create a new one, one which will be appropriate for the new object. In short, *accomodation* refers to the tendency to act, feel, and think as the situation demands. Thus, in assimilating an object into our preexistent cognitive structure, we transform the object to fit our structures as they are, without changing them. By contrast, when it is necessary to transform our own pre-existing cognitive structures to know an object, we are accommodating. As we have said earlier, the entire process involves *differentiation,* creating separate schemata for objects that do not fit pre-existing schemata; as well as *integration,* relating schemata to one another in an effort to expand our pre-existing ones. These two processes are complimentary. In the development of intellect both assimilatory and accommodatory processes are necessarily involved. As I pointed out earlier, the inherited human tendency to balance knowledge gained through assimilation with knowledge which results from accomodations is termed *equilibration.*

To summarize, organization and adaptation are functional invariants that are inherited human tendencies. Organization refers to the tendency to create meaningful wholes out of segments of knowledge, and adaptation is the tendency to adjust. Adaptation takes the form of either acting as previously experienced (assimilation) or acting in new ways depending upon the immediate situation (accommodation).

THE CONCEPT OF STAGE

When the structures of knowledge within an individual are integrated in such a way that they give rise to a consistent pattern of acting and thinking, we can speak of *stage*. Each stage consistutes a unique structure of thought, a unique pattern of action and thought. The entire course of human intellectual development is characterized by the construction of stages that are qualitatively different from one another. Each stage is superior—in kind, not in degree—from its predecessor. Flavell (1963) states that for Piaget the concept is a necessary as well as a justified one because there is "sufficient qualitative homogeneity . . . [among children of similar ages] to permit such analysis (p. 19)." Stated otherwise, there seems to be enough intellectual similarity among children of roughly the same age, and enough intellectual differences between them and children of other ages to warrant speaking of stages. Having established the reality of stages in intellectual development, we can now speak of its properties. Inhelder (1962) has summarized the properties of stages as follows:

First, Piaget views intellectual development as a process of progressive change in the structures of action and thought. This process has a period of formation and a period of actualization. The recurrent regularity of mental operations points to the organized (and equilibrated) nature of thinking which is characteristic of the *end* of a given stage. For instance, children in the stage of sensorimotor intelligence know the world by pulling, pushing, grasping, sucking objects. The end of this stage, which coincides roughly with the end of the child's second birthday, is characterized by a mastery of knowing the world of reality by performing these functions upon it in an organized way. This knowledge structure provides a regularity of action which is the same for all children in this stage the world over. It is this universal pattern of action that necessitates invoking the concept of stage.

Second, each stage consists of qualitatively different structures of action and thought. This point is important because it emphasizes that transformation in intellectual structurings is not a matter of degree but a matter of kind, i.e., the *type* of structurings are different from stage to stage. Yet, the attainment of one stage signals the beginning of the next. In moving from one stage to the next, the child's preceding structures are subsumed and integrated into the newly constructed structures. In this sense, older structures are not disposed of, they are built upon.

By the end of the second birthday, and for a period of approximately five years, the child is progressing from a stage in which his actions were limited to the sensorimotoric world to a stage in which the emerging abilities of symbolizing reality is being mastered. In the second stage, or the preoperational stage, the child is busily building upon his newly developed powers of representation—powers that will free him from the "hands-on" physical form of knowing to a way of knowing that is characterized by language, mental imagery and imaginative play. It is precisely these powers of representation that are forming and improving during this stage. The fact that children begin to speak during this period, and because of the peculiar and highly intuitive form of reasoning that children the world over manifest during this period, is evidence enough to warrant speaking of the concept of stage.

Third, the developmental process is viewed as unalterable, i.e., the various stages of development manifest themselves in an orderly and fixed manner. Here we are saying that the structure of intellect follows a lawful sequence—certain structures must be attained before higher level structures can be constructed. This simply means that a child must attain one stage before he/she can proceed to the next. The child cannot jump over one stage. Every stage must be attained completely before we can begin to think, feel, and act with the "tools" of the next higher stage. However, this does not mean that once we have attained a stage we never return to that stage. As a matter of fact, we never fully abandon any stage, not even the sensori-motoric one. For example, when I ask adults to describe a spiral staircase, they almost always revert to a sensori-motoric gesture of twirling their forefinger in the air in an upward motion indicating a spiral. Also, it is quite evident to adults that when they confront a novel problem, they tend to view it from an intuitive, perceptual basis, even though they are quite capable of abstract thinking. We tend to concretize abstract phenomena with which we are not very familiar.

Fourth, even though the order of appearance of the various stages are invariant, the tempo of achieving the various stages may be increased or retarded. That is to say, it is possible for children of the same age to be in different stages of intellectual development. Recall that Piaget is an interactionist, and as such, he places due emphasis on experiential aspects of children's lives. Thus, children in different cultures—and even in the same ones—can differ in the speed with which they move through the various stages of intellectual development. This is not to say that direct instruction over a relatively short duration of time will increase the tempo of attainment, rather it is to say that the cultural milieu (including the quality of long-term experiences) can influence the speed of attainment. To coin a phrase, it is a matter of construction, not a matter of instruction. Thus, age does not determine stage. Some 6 year-olds may already be concrete thinkers while others are still struggling with concepts requiring concrete logic. Still some 15 year-olds are formal thinkers and some are not. Here it is interesting to note that cross-cultural research has shown certain patterns of differences in intellectual development that shed some light on this issue. For example, it has been shown that the closer the culture is to a western, industrialized, and urbanized one, the more favorable it is to children's intellectual development. More specifically, it has been shown that urban children attain the certain stages at younger ages than do rural children, regardless of the culture within which the comparison is made. Furthermore, children of remote cultures tend to lag behind schooled children who are urbanized (Dasen, 1977). All of this supports the notion that the tempo for attaining stages is not fixed, that the tempo can be influenced by the cultural setting in which one lives.

Summary And Implications: How Can These Factors Be Influenced?

Intellectual development depends on the interaction of four factors: maturation, social transmission, physical experience and equilibration. While together these factors are necessary and sufficient in explaining the actualization of human intellectual development, no single factor alone is sufficient. The process of equilibration is the motivational factor behind cognitive adaptations. The equilibration process propels the organism to achieve higher forms of adaptations through two functional invariants, organization and adaptation. The tendency for organization ultimately results in logically consistent and coherent patterns of thought giving rise to more adaptative and flexible thought. Intellectual adaptation can occur either by assimilating objects of knowledge into pre-existing organization, or by accommodating (changing) these structures when the external stimulus situation demands it. Here intellectual adaptation is equated with intelligence and it ultimately leads to higher and higher levels of organized knowledge.

The concept of intellectual structure holds a central position in Piaget's theory as it does in other theories as well, e.g., Gestalt psychology. However, the difference between other structural accounts of human functioning and Piaget's lies in the latter's insistence that the laws governing structures are not synchronic, but diachronic. Since structures are governed by laws that are time-dependent or diachronic, it becomes encumbent upon Piaget to describe how these structures do in fact change as a function of time. Such accounts ultimately hinge on the role of equilibration, a self-regulatory mechanism of the actions of the subject. In essence, this intrinsic, or built-in, mechanism tends to react to any disturbances from without the subject. The objective of these self-regulatory reactions is to adjust the subject's momentary state of equilibrium to physical and social experiences. The systematic ways in which we adjust to our physical and social world define coherent structures. Attempts to describe such structures resulted in Piaget's concept of stage or intellectual development with the following features: (1) intellectual development is a process of progressive integrations of the structures of action and thought resulting in four stages, (2) each stage consists of qualitatively different structures of action and thought, (3) the developmental process is viewed as unalterable, and (4) the tempo of attainment of the various stages may be increased or retarded.

The educational implications related to the issues discussed in this chapter may now be summarized. Since intellectual development is a spontaneous process which results from the factors of maturation, physical experience, social transmission, and equilibration, it can be influenced by long-term educational and social interventions. For example, long-term (and particularly very early) education can directly affect changes in the factors of maturation. To the extent that such intervention includes nutritional components especially for the unborn baby (through the mother's diet), to that extent the factor of maturation can be somewhat influenced—influenced only in the sense of enabling it to achieve its hereditary potential. In terms of physical experience, education can strive to provide objects of knowledge upon which students can act. Once again the reader is reminded that "objects of knowledge" can include concrete, physical objects but is certainly not limited to these. Objects of knowledge include physical objects, abstract concepts, feelings, beliefs, mental processes, etc. In fact, the phrase refers to anything that can be potentially known. The educationally significant point is that a wide variety of such "objects" must be made available, and that such objects must be selected to correspond to the student's stage of intellectual development. Furthermore, as Bruner (1966) has pointed out, physical experience should ideally begin with *enactive* manipulations, or motoric, first-hand experiences; then proceed to *iconic,* or representational manipulation (as in using pictures, diagrams, caricatures, etc.); and finally to the *symbolic* mode of knowing, in which manipulations of words, numbers, signs, concepts, formulae, etc. Knowledge is best acquired through action. To be consistent with Piaget's constructivism, students should be allowed to act on objects of knowledge in spontaneous ways, all in an effort to discover the properties of such objects and at the same time to invent new ways of acting (logico-mathematical knowledge). But not all knowledge is discovered and invented. Some forms of knowledge are simply *accepted*. For example, we learn that we must drive on a certain side of the road, to stop at a red light and go when it turns green; we learn our culture's way of dressing, of conducting ourselves as citizens, as guests, as studnets, as professionals, etc. The object of knowledge in all of these learnings is a social convention, based on concensual agreement as opposed to scientific research and logic. Other examples of this form of knowledge include the socially-defined conventions of spelling, typing, ritualistic behavior, etc. In general, knowledge that is the product of social opinion, concensus and convention can be directly transmitted, it need not be discovered. Equilibration too can be influenced by education, but of course only in an indirect manner. For example, often it is possible to indirectly influence it through dialectics. That is, students' knowledge can often be upset by the teacher through the introduction of questions, problems, objects, events, etc., that contradict students' knowledge. This generally results in a motivation to assimilate the new knowledge into old schemata. The motivation is intrinsic, because equilibration seeks better forms of equilibrium. When what is new cannot be fitted into the old schemata, accommodation results. Thus, equilibration can indeed be influenced by creating the conditions that result in the student's questioning of his current knowledge. The "training studies" recently reported by Inhelder, Sinclair, and Bovet (1974) showed that the strategy of disequilibrating a student's knowledge will result in self-correction of some very fundamental competencies when the student is in transition from one stage of development to the next. That is, these researchers have shown that under certain conditions the strategy of de-stabilizing a student's knowledge can lead to self-correction. But like any strategy, its effects are limited, limited by the factors of maturation, physical experience, and social transmission.

The crucial concepts of assimilation and accommodation likewise suggest particular educational practice. These concepts suggest that the student's first cognitive impulse is to relate a given educational experience to what he already knows. Thus, educational practice should recognize this tendency, and can increase its effectiveness by inventing

54

ways in which it begins with what is already known by the student. The idea of providing "advance organizers" (Ausubel, 1963) is a case in point. Recent research on comprehension also supports the view that "contexts" that are provided before instruction proper enhances comprehension (Bransford, 1979).

Additionally, assimilation requires self-initiated repetition. That is, once an object of knowledge has been assimilated, there is a tendency to use the newly acquired knowledge and to apply it in a variety of situations. It is therefore important that students be given opportunity to sufficiently exercise their newly acquired knowledge as well as to transfer it to other situations. Once again recent research confirms this principle, but the kind of exercise that we are talking about is not one of repeating the newly acquired action without regard to the underlying principle(s) involved. For example, Thune and Eriksen (1978) have shown that students who are given practice in solving problems on a calculator do better, than students who have been told about how all calculators work, on those problems using those particular calculators. But when new calculators are given to the students to solve those problems, the students who were told about the principles of all calculators do better. Thus, endeavors to teach transfer of learning should emphasize the general type of transfer know as "learning to learn," or how to transfer a process, not just a learned product.

The process of accommodation is usually more difficult for students for they are required to change in some way, to create new schemata, new ways of organizing knowledge. Accommodation naturally requires the student to adjust his old ways of knowing. This is quite challenging, and if students have had sufficient assimilatory experiences they will not resist the change; otherwise, the resistance may be acute. Teachers can gain a great deal of knowledge of their students when they carefully observe how students are reacting to new objects of knowledge. A great deal of resistance usually suggests insufficient assimilatory experience.

Finally, the concept of stage (as described in the preceding pages) leads us to the following educationally relevant points. Since age is only a rough indicator of stage of development, it is best to use the concept of stage, as opposed to age, in formulating educational experiences. Second, progress from one stage to another is a gradual matter, one which cannot be accelerated by short-term, specialized instruction. Transformation in intellectual structurings are subject to *time* restrictions and cannot be accelerated at will. Students must be given plenty of opportunity to spontaneously interact with "curriculum."

The British primary schools are the best examples of how this can be done (see Blackie, 1967). Thirdly, students cannot be expected to act abstractly with respect to a given object of knowledge just because they have shown that they can act abstractly with other objects of knowledge. Intellectual structures interact with content. If a learner has a great deal of assimilatory experience with a given content, then we can expect more advanced mental manipulations on that content. The student may not be able to spontaneously use these mental manipulations on different (non-familiar content) content. Finally, to teach children the experimental tasks that define a given stage of development is to misuse the theory. Such teachings do not ordinarily result in any qualitative changes in the students' cognitive functioning, only in their surface manifestations.

---

* The phase "objects of knowledge" refers to all things that can be known by a knower.
** Informal talk in Columbia, Maryland.   [Chapter 4B]

5 Development, Learning, and Motivation

In this chapter I would like to consider three interrelated concepts that are central to any discussion of education, passive or active. I am speaking here of the concepts of intellectual development, learning, and cognitive motivation.

Intellectual Development

By now it is perhaps intuitively clear what we mean by intellectual or cognitive development. Cognitive development refers to the process by which subjects structure their activities as they interact with their social and physical environments. This process is viewed as an extension of biological development. More specifically, in his book entitled *Structuralism,* Piaget (1971) draws an analogy between cognitive development and biological epigenesis. Kitchener (1978) has summarized the essential features to the process of epigenesis as follows: (a) a causal *sequence* of events is involved; (b) this sequence of events is characterized by increasing differentiation, integration, and *complexity*; (c) with increasing complexity, differentiation, and integration, a *new state* emerges; and (d) these newly emergent states constitute *stages* that are structurally (qualitatively) different from each other.

As we have already seen, Piaget maintains that: (a) intellectual development is characterized by a sequence of action and thought; (b) that these actions and thoughts become organized at higher phases, becoming more flexible and mobile; (c) that they encompass previous actions and emerge as new states or modes of acting and thinking; and (d) that these newly constructed modes of action and thought constitute intellectual stages (sensorimotor, preoperational, concrete operational, and formal operational). The parallel between biological epigenesis and intellectual development is not accidental.

Intellectual development is first and foremost a structuring activity that is intrinsic to the knowing person. As the person acts upon, and interacts with, his environment, he structures his actions into a general form. This general *form* of acting (physically as well as mentally) constitutes intelligence. The natural evolution of this general form of acting over the course of the various stages constitutes intellectual development. The factors that affect this development are maturation, physical experience, social transmission, and equilibration. It is the nature of the interaction among these factors that determines the form of acting and thinking for any given person. To the extent that the biological mechanisms are normal and developing adequately (maturation), and there are adequate and varied physical experience as well as social/cultural interchange, we would expect natural intellectual development.

Development And Learning

Now that we have a better idea of what is meant by cognitive development, let us look at what Piaget has meant by learning. First, we must recognize that the construct of learning has never occupied a central position in genetic epistemology. Learning has always occupied a secondary position in Piaget's developmental constructivism. As such, Piaget has said little regarding this problem. In a series of two papers entitled "Apprentissage et connaissance," Piaget (1959a, 1959b) distinguishes between two forms of learning: physical learning and logico-mathematical learning, and in a published address (Piaget, 1964), he draws a distinction between development and learning. In other works, Piaget makes minor statements regarding learning as contrasted with instinct, etc. (see Gruber & Vonèche [eds], 1977). Let us turn first to the distinction between learning and development.

LEARNING AND DEVELOPMENT: A DISTINCTION

In distinguishing between learning and development, Piaget (1964) makes a number of points. First, he reminds us that the development of knowledge, in the general sense, is spontaneous. What does he mean by spontaneous? Clearly "spontaneous" refers to activity " . . . in its general biological and psychological context (p. 38)." Any artificial provocation, any ecologically invalid intrusion, is interpreted to be non-spontaneous. In this sense, learning is the opposite of development. "In general, learning is provoked by situations— provoked by a psychological experimenter; or by a teacher, with respect to some didactic points; or by an external situation (p. 38)." So the first feature of learning, when contrasted with development, is that it is provoked while development is spontaneous. A second feature in this distinction lies in the limited nature of learning. By and large, learning is "limited to a single problem, or to a single structure (p. 38)," while development is not. A third feature of learning is that it is determined by development, and not vice versa. A given experience may or may not result in learning depending upon the subject's level of cognitive development. Thus, the impact of experience (learning) is dependent upon the already existing intellectual structures of the subject (cognitive development).

An example may help to put these three points in perspective. Is it possible to teach five year-olds that no matter how we change the shape of a chunk of clay that we have not changed its weight? This type of learning requires certain developmental competencies, including quantitative reversibility. We put two chunks of clay on a balance and show that they weigh the same. We ask what would happen if we change the shape of one of the chunks, say into a sausage or a pancake. The children insist that the sausage or the pancake is "bigger" and therefore it would weigh more. We explain that we didn't add any clay to either side, but that doesn't change their minds. So we make the sausage and put it back on the scale. The children can't believe the results: no difference in weight. So we proceed along these lines, creating innumerable transformations on the clay. The results always show the same thing: no matter how we change the shape of the clay, the weight stays the same. Soon, we conclude that the children "learned" the concept of conservation of weight. After all, they predict that the weight will be the same no matter what transformation is performed on it. Yet, when we conduct a rigorous test of this learning, we find that it was artificial. If we steal a piece of the clay and ask for a prediction: we will receive what we taught; namely, that the two sides will weigh the same. When we put the clay (with the missing piece) back on the scale, the scale tips. The children are startled. How can this be? When we inquire further as to how would this outcome be explained, the result is interesting—the children revert back to their old notions of preconservation of weight; namely, they say that the balance should be tipping because this piece is shorter, smaller, flatter, etc. It is crucial for our present discussion to note that seven or eight year-old conservers, when put through a similar test conclude that "something is fishy." They will not revert to preconservationist notions to explain a contradictory outcome.

Thus, Piaget (1964) argues that learning is a function of development, i.e., development can explain learning but learning cannot explain development. In short, one can learn a given phenomenon, if and only if, his developmental stage is sufficiently advanced so that the mental operations that are demanded of the learning task are already within his or her grasp. If a college student is trying to *learn* the concept of simple relatively, we might expect his reasoning to have *developed* to a point where he can coordinate two systems of reference. Conversely, and on a lower level, no matter how hard we try to teach a child that a pound of feathers weighs the same as a pound of rocks, he will not learn! He will insist that a pound of rocks weighs more. This *developmental* limitation determines the *learning,* or in this case, the impossibility of learning. As I have pointed out earlier, we can expect learning experiences to contribute to cognitive development only when a match between cognitive structure and a particular experience is made (Piaget, 1970).

The second distinction that Piaget makes is between two forms of learning, both of which stem from interacting with the physical world. Knowledge formation is dependent upon the nature of the interaction of the subject with the object of knowledge. There are essentially two types of objects with which one can interact: (a) the physical world, and (b) the social world. In terms of the subject's interactions with the physical world, two kinds of experiences are possible: (a) direct physical experience, and (b) logical-mathematical experience. Each of these types of experience gives rise to a different form of abstraction, hence to a different type of learning. These two forms of learning have been labelled P (direct physical) and LM (logico-mathematical) learning (Piaget, 1959a; 1959b).*

We have alluded to these two forms of abstractions earlier in this book. An example may be useful in clarifying this critical distinction. In playing with candy a child discovers that it is sweet, it is solid, it melts gradually, etc. In this case the child has experienced and has learned something about the physical properties of this type of candy (P learning). In the same vein, when the child discovers that a piece of candy can be hurled and a feather cannot, that a piece of candy is heavier than the feather, etc., he also has learned something about the physical properties of candy. On the other hand, when the child groups all the yellow candies in one pile, the green in another, etc., or when he arranges them from largest to smallest, or when he realizes that the number of candies remains the same despite the fact that they may be spread out or put into a pile, he is in fact engaged in a wholly different activity. This type of activity is also a product of the child's interaction with the objects of knowledge, but it results in knowledge about one's own thinking. The resulting abstractions from such experience Piaget labels "LM or logico-mathematical learning." LM learning is essentially a construction of one's own intellectual actions upon objects of knowledge, the resultant of which is learning, not so much about properties of objects *per se,* but about properties of one's own thinking processes. The intellectual acts resulting in classification, (grouping according to certain criteria) seriation (ordering objects along certain dimensions), conservation (realizing that a transformation performed on an object can be reversed), etc., are all logico-mathematical in nature. But how does this form of knowledge evolve into more sophisticated forms, forms that are more complex, flexible and mobile?

THE FOLE OF STRUCTURAL LEARNING IN DEVELOPMENT

As I have pointed out in Chapter Three, the main problem of theories of knowledge (empiricism, nativism, constructivism) is the appearance and evolution of new knowledge. It will be recalled that for Piaget neither empiricism nor nativism addresses the question of the construction of new structures of knowledge. Piaget accepts neither the view that structures are discovered ready-made by virtue of experience (empiricism), nor the view that these logico-mathematical structures are *pre*formed prior to experience. As we have seen social-cultural transmission as well as physical experience do play important roles in the formation and evolution of logical structures, but they are not sufficient in explaining such development. This is so for two reasons. First, experience is not a copy of reality, it is a personal phenomenon for it must be assimilated through the actions of the subject; hence for adaptation to take place, actions must be integrated, coordinated with one another to form a noncontradictory whole. Since these experiences are not haphazardly added together, some factor must be postulated to account for this integration and coordination, a factor that is inherent in these actions themselves and that regulates them. Second, social transmission cannot account for the formation and evolution of logical structures either, for we must ask where did society get these structures in the first place and how can the child understand them. Thus, a third factor was postulated by Piaget to account for this fact of integration, coordination, and continuous reorganization. Piaget (1971) termed this factor *equilibration*. As we have seen in Chapter 4, equilibration is a dynamic process of self-regulations of the actions of the subject. Piaget (1970, p. 725) conceives of equilibration "as a set of active reactions of the subject to external disturbances, which can be effective, or anticipated to varying degrees." As we saw earlier, a "stage" of intellectual development is characterized by a set of logical structures which are said to be in a momentary state of equilibrium. A given experience, a provocation, may cause a "disturbance" or a perturbation in this equilibrated state. Disequilibrium may result. And as we have seen, disequilibrium motivates the subject to readjust, to re-establish another (higher) level of (momentary) equilibrium. This time the new state of equilibrium can deal with the disturbance that caused it to expand. The result is progress. We now have a more complex, flexible and mobile set of intellectual operations. The new state of equilibrium can assimilate more diverse experiences now, as well as accommodate to a wider variety of events.

Thus far we have seen how the factors of maturation, physical experience, social transmission, and equilibration affect structural learning which in turn may affect intellectual development. However, the factors of social transmission and physical experience affect not only the general mode of spontaneous activity (intelligence), but also the specific and acquired information (a kind of learning). These factors not only affect the *form* of the activity itself, but also its *content*.

LEARNING THROUGH SOCIAL TRANSMISSION

To the behaviorist, learning consists of a relatively lasting change in behavior that comes about through practice (some say reinforced practiced). Certainly, one can witness change in behavior (performance) as a result of practice. Acquisition of physical skills, much of our learning that occurs through social transmission, our daily habits, etc. can be reduced to this definition. In other words, much of what is learned can be attributed to socially transmitted (instructed) forms of experience. This type of learning is information-specific, it is specific to a given set of socially or culturally determined circumstances. This type of learning results in acquisition of contents of thought. We can learn through instruction all the ready-made knowledge of our culture: spelling, English history, rules of the road, law, names and dates of events, etc. This kind of learning is peculiar to the social group to which we belong. None of it characterizes all of humanity, it does not contribute to the universal *forms* of knowledge that are said to underly the stages of intellectual development.

In this sense, learning is information-specific, while development is human-specific. In other words, learning is specific to the *contents* of thought, while development refers to the specifically human *processes* of thought. For example, while I may know what water is, what a glass is, etc. (content-specific knowledge), I may not know that I can pour water from one type of container (narrow and long) to another (shallow and short) and still have the same amount of water; or that I can belong to two classes of things at the same time, e.g., be Jewish and an American at the same time (although these concepts are obvious for the adult, children in certain stages of development have not yet developed them). This type of knowledge characterizes what we have called "human-specific." Information-specific knowledge is also susceptible to the laws of forgetting. Learning that is brought about by social transmission is easily forgotten unless it is repeatedly used.

On the other hand, the development of operations is not susceptible to forgetting. For example, the development of the operation of reversibility enables children to "see" that transferring liquid problem by simply retracing steps to achieve the original state of the liquod. In sum, the content of thought resulting from developmental processes encompasses those attained through learning processes.

Cognitive Motivation

Piaget's theory of cognitive motivation rests on the construct of *equilibration* (Piaget and Inhelder, 1969). Briefly, equilibration refers to the self-regulatory mechanism which attempts to balance assimilatory tendencies with accommodatory activity. It will be recalled that assimilation refers to the predisposition to act cognitively as the subject has acted in the past, to incorporate an object of knowledge into already-existing schemata; whereas accommodation refers to the requirement, imposed by an obtrusive stimulus, to act in response to it, to create new schemata. Equilibration is the underlying motivation to strike a balance between these two aspects of cognitive activity.

Thus, the theory proposes two factors which contribute to cognitive motivation: the first being a by-product of assimilatory activity, the second stemming from the necessity to admit compelling and obtrusive stimuli that impinge on the subject. In the first instance, Piaget has shown that as cognitive structures are formulated they tend to function; i.e., to be exercised (functional assimilation). That is to say that the act of assimilation carries with it a motive to relate what one is presently encountering with what one already knows. The tendency to relate new to old is automatic. Secondly, if fairly well-balanced structures are challenged by conflicting evidence as when the subject cannot relate the new to the old, then he feels compelled to regulate the new information. This cognitive motivation, stimulated by mental conflict, activates and directs the subject to balance assimilatory with accommodatory activity, in an effort to resolve conflicts in mental structures. This aspect of cognitive motivation was investigated in a series of learning experiments by Inhelder, Sinclair, and Bovet (1974) in which the effect of various forms of conflict (verbal, demonstrative, etc.) upon the reasoning of subjects was studied. These researchers discovered that when the conflict source is physical evidence that contradicts the subject's prediction of a certain outcome, then he is likely to modify his reasoning in favor of higher levels of explanation.

Obviously, the subject must be mature enough to recognize the conflict in the first place or else the strategy is useless.

Recently it has also been shown that cognitive conflict induced by peers does have a positive effect on children's acquisition of certain concepts (Perret-Clermont, 1976). In short, cognitive motivation is intrinsic and adaptive with two facets: (a) to relate new knowledge to what is already known, and (b) to resolve conflict that is created by a lack of fit between new and compelling information and old cognitive structures.

Apparently, the equilibration process may be characterized in terms of an ongoing dialecticism (Piaget, 1950): contradiction in thought, either stemming out of physical evidence or out of the inferential process of the thinker, propels thought to seek more mature forms of functioning.

It should be noted that cognitive conflict does not result unless the subject is capable of recognizing the inconsistency giving rise to such conflict. For example, when children of various ages are asked whether a pound of clay is heavier than a pound of feathers they react differently. The very young (preoperational) child responds by saying that the clay is heavier. In this case the child shows no signs of confusion and no conflict. He appears pleased with his answer. On the other hand, an older child may be upset by the question itself, realizing that a "trick" may be involved, but he is unsure of what it is. This child may answer with some hesitation. And if his answer happens to be in error, he will tend to show signs of disturbance. This child has assimilated aspects of the problem but is not fully capable of reversibility which is required to successfully answer this question. Conflict in mental structures motivates the child to seek a closure to this problem. In the next few months the child may resolve this conflict, given appropriate maturation, physical and social experiences. the fact that the child attains reversibility to the point of comprehending the problem and providing the correct answer does not mean that the child's motivation will cease. Numerous other problems, dilemmas, etc., will be raised in the meantime, given adequate physical and social stimulation.

In summary, Piaget's (1950) conception of motivation is inextricably related to intellectual adaptation. This is obviously so because in order for the subject to adapt he must interact with the environment. This interaction is intrinsic to the subject's intelligence for without such interaction adaptation would not be possible. Thus, the subject has an inherent motive to engage in activities that lead to higher and higher forms of adaptation. Once structures are formed, there is a predisposition toward utilizing them. This predisposition is a fundamental aspect of cognitive life. Again, this is obvious from the standpoint of Piaget's conception of assimilatory processes: assimilation requires self-initiated repetition. On the other hand, once a structure has been functionally assimilated to the point of equilibrium, the subject tends to lose interest in exercising it. Evidence regarding this contention comes from various sources and is manifested clearly in studies into the role of *surprise* in cognitive motivation. For example, Charlesworth (1969) has demonstrated that subjects tended to remain at tasks which presented them with an element of surprise. Other researchers, e.g., Berlyne (1965) have shown that tasks involving moderate novelty were the most interesting to subjects, while tasks (or stimuli) that were mundane or totally discrepant to the subject's previous cognitions were not as interesting to them.

THE PROBLEM OF THE MATCH

The principle of moderate novelty is clearly related to the "problem of the match" (Hunt, 1961), which is crucial to the proper motivation of the student. Essentially the problem requires the matching of materials, readings, problems, etc., that the educator makes available to his students with those students' levels of comprehension. The problem of the match, as an ongoing educational endeavor, is at the heart of the educator's tasks. As you can see, ideally, the educator must have an adequate grasp of the intellectual structures and functions of his students, and in reality, he must have a least a framework which describes the type of student he is attempting to teach.** In addition, the educator must have an understanding of curriculum materials and activities that are appropriate for those structures and functions. This is an enormously complicated task. However, it should be remembered that failure to successfully address the problem of the match results either in boredom (if the tasks require already well-exercised structures) or in rote learning (if the tasks require mental activity that is yet not under the control of the learner). In either case, the subject will not be motivated to know and will learn little if anything at all.

Finally, it should be stressed that for Piaget every intellectual act consists of a structural (logical) component as well as an affective (emotive) component. Having acted, the subject renders a value judgment regarding his action: the act is judged on a continuum of "good-bad." This must indeed be so because adaptation is the continual goal of intelligence. Therefore, adaptability is the criterion for making this value judgment. In short, acts of intelligence are judged by that intelligence as adaptive (good) or not adaptive (bad). Thus, the motivation toward intellectual adaptation must be considered to be intrinsic to the individual. The growth of intelligence is governed not only by the influence of factors that lie outside the knower, the external world, but also by a force from within the knower himself. This internal factor which Piaget has called *equilibration* is the heart of cognitive motivation.

Given this motivational theory, a number of educational principles present themselves. First, the principle of assimilation requiring repetition leads to the educational implication that subjects need to exercise (practice) the knowledge which they have recently constructed. Practice is a necessary element in the acquisition of information and the construction of knowledge. It should be emphasized that if what is newly acquired is meaningful to the subject, i.e., if he can relate the new to the old, the subject will *want* to practice.

Secondly, the educator must recognize signs of intellectual disturbances, as when the subject is in a state of mental conflict. Ordinarily such conflict signifies an attempt to comprehend. The subject may ask hard questions at this point. The educator must be able to recognize when these questions are legitimate to the subject and when they are merely directed toward intellectually illegitimate aims. Conflict of the sort we have been referring to usually refers to periods of transition in intellectual structures. Thus, is should be expected that, at this time, the subject will waver back and forth on a certain issue. This wavering usually manifests itself in honest questioning as well as in uncertainty; the subject may "know" today, but not tomorrow. This transition period is crucial to the learner and he must be supported and encouraged. Unfortunately, this is a trying period for the educator who often interprets these questions as a challenge of his authority. If the educational atmosphere is one in which the educator is perceived as a guide in the learning process as opposed to a transmitter of knowledge, then feelings of challenge and threat on the part of the educator will be minimized.

Thirdly, the principle of the moderately novel directs the educator toward the problem of the match. The educator must resolve this problem. The solution is obviously a task of enormous proportions, requiring the joint efforts of teachers, educational and child psychologists, curriculum specialists, and school psychologists. The task begins with a thorough grounding in genetic cognitive psychology as well as in a working knowledge of curriculum materials and activities. Ultimately these two aspects must be combined such that the available learning activities and materials may be appropriate for learners of varying intellectual competencies. Often, the educator may find himself using an individualized instructional mode to accomplish this task.

But, the problem of the match is not reducable to the problem of how to individualize instruction. Various grouping techniques based on "developmental age" (as opposed to chronological age), and some that overlap children of various ages (vertical grouping) have also been successfully used to reach a solution to this problem.

The question of the match is notmerely one which has motivational implications. It is a problem that deals with the crucial issue of what is learned. In essence, the problem of the match is a problem of recognizing what is already known so that a match can be created.

Some Educational Implications

Piaget (1961) makes it clear that cognitive development is not solely dependent upon learning, either in the direct physical sense or in the logico-mathematical sense; cognitive development requries interaction of the factors of maturation, social transmission, and equilibration as well (Piaget, 1961). It is development then that sets the boundaries of *what* in the physical world can be directly experienced and *how* that object will be experienced. Thus, development determines learning and not the converse.

Since we as educators are in the business of constructing environments that promote *learning*, we must recognize the developmental attainments and limitations of our students. To be more specific, for example, most 5 and 6 year-olds cannot conserve quantity (e.g., number). That is, they do not recognize that a number will remain constant despite certain transformations performed on that number. For example, most 5 and 6 year-olds do not realize that a certain number of candies will remain that number no matter whether one piles them together or distributes them apart. Without knowledge of this psychological limitation, we might insist on teaching children to add and subtract. If we do, learning will take place, but it will certainly be a rote type of learning. In general then, we must have in mind, at least a description of the epistemic subject's (if not of the actual subject's) attainments and limitations, for then we can choose what our students learn more intelligently. Whereas meaningful learning *can* take place when development permits, rote learning *will* take place when development does not permit. As a guide to what development will permit and what it won't, we can certainly turn to Piaget's description of the epistemic subject (i.e., his description of the knower as he moves from one stage of intellectual development to the next). In addition, the distinction between development and learning clearly shows that some aspects of physical learning can be directly influenced by the teacher, but logico-mathematical learning cannot be so influenced. Logico-

mathematical learning can only be indirectly influenced insofar as we have an adequate understanding of the stage of the knower's conceptual level and are able to arrange educational materials which give rise to such learning.
motivation.

* A more elaborate treatment of this discussion will appear in Chapter Four.
** We shall return to this problem of the "typical" student later on in this paper.

Chapter 5b

6 Piagetian Education: Some Principles

To begin with, Piaget (1972a, p. 137) defines his methods as

> those that take account of the child's own peculiar nature
> and make their appeal to the individual's psychological
> constitution and those of his development. Passivity as
> against activity.

As you can see, the appeal is one of moving away from intuitive education and on to an education that has its foundation in knowledge about the psychological (and more specifically, the psycholgentic) makeup of the student.

In contrast to passive methods, active methods are based on a psychological picture of intellectual development. These methods attempt to build on what is evidenced in children during the first few years of life: an intrinsic curiosity to know, an eagerness to observe and explain, inquire and construct, explore and discover, invent and test. In these acts lies the intellectual foundation for all that will follow. In particular, the prototypes of logico-mathematical abilities to compare and contrast, categorize and arrange, count and verify, as well as the prototypes of scientific abilities (abilities of explaining causes, correlations, and functional relationships) are all present very early in life. It is therefore the task of the new methods to create conditions that enable the learner to extend these abilities. The following constitute a limited set of educational implications directly stemming from the constructivist view of intellectual development. As such these implications represent some fundamental principles of active, or Piagetian education.

Some Principles Of Active Education

First and foremost, educators must develop as thorough an understanding of the principles of genetic cognitive psychology as possible. This is an indispensable requirement in active education for it offers the educator a framework of students' intellectual attainments and limitations. For example, it is a hopeless and frustrating task to teach college freshmen the principle of simple relativity if they do not, or cannot, reason by using systems of reference. On the lower grades, it is once again hopeless to engage elementary school children in formal inferential logic for they tend to interpret the premise as having to be empirically true, when it need not be, and they can't keep track of the deductions that would be possible given that premise. Further down, we encounter the child who cannot conserve quantity, yet we demand that he learn that multiplication and division are inverse processes; or even further down the scale of intellectual development when we insist that the child learn to discriminate "cow" from "doggie" when he insists on categorizing all four-legged animals as "bow-wow"! The world of education would be so much simpler if educators (parents, teachers, curriculum writers, principals) recognized the *real* intellectual capabilities and limitations that characterizes their learners. Equipped with this knowledge, the educator can engage students in relatively meaningful educational activity as well as having a reference for understanding their language and actions in regard to those activities.

A second principle that can be constructed is focused on the student. *The student must be given a choice of tasks that engage him or her actively, both physically and mentally, in the sense that the tasks permit manipulations, explorations, rediscoveries, and reinventions on the part of the student.* Generally speaking, activity does not imply the exclusion of tasks that do not have a manual or a psychomotor component. This is a narrow interpretation that is often misunderstood. As I said earlier, activity can have broader meanings, to include mental manipulations of objects, events, or acts. As Piaget (1972a, p. 27) puts it: "a student may be totally 'active,' in the sense of making a personal rediscovery of the truths to be acquired, even though this activity is being directed toward interior and abstract reflection." What is called upon, therefore, is active learning, not active teaching. For the teacher, certainly teaching is an active method of learning because it places the burden of gatherings, synthesizing, organizing, relating, and communicating information on the teacher. All of these activities must be the domain of the learner. When the teacher is the active agent, the learner is restricted to the less active modes such as listening, watching, attending, and following directions.

In his remarkable book, Seymore Papert (1980) introduces the concept of syntonic learning, i.e., learning that is based on a relation between the self and the to-be-known object. So if the first rule in Piagetian learning is syntonicity, then its primary corollary is *body syntonicity,* or basing the new learning on the learner's knowledge of his own body. In short, to the extent that we can related new learning to what one body already does, then the easier the learning will be.

Active manipulation of objects concretizes the learning, making assimilation so much more easier.

Active education is based on the assumption that individuals tend to seek to interact meaningfully with their environment. To the extent that a match can be struck between the student's conceptual level and the intellectual demands of an educational activity, there will be a meaningful interaction. Meaningful interaction with the environment as well as with one's own abstractions of that environment is an intrinsic aspect of the knowing process.

Thus, a third principle of active education lies in the continual effort on the part of the educator to provide students with educational opportunities that match their interests and their cognitive abilities. Without such effort, the selection of "curriculum" materials becomes intuitive and may lead to rote learning (in cases where the material is above the student's conceptual level) or to boredom (if the material is below that level). Thus, active education must strive to accommodate itself to children who are functioning on varying intellectual planes so that they can all assimilate aspects of the new knowledge. In this way, knowledge can be a personal appropriation; each student assimilating aspects of his educational experience in a personal way. We all tend to relate what we are trying to comprehend to what we already know. This relating process (or assimilatory activity) is at the heart of the knowledge acquisition process; it is an intrinsic aspect of learning and knowing. In other words, children create meaning by relating the new to the old, by relating that which they are trying to understand to that which they already understand. This is true of infants, young children, middle childhood, adolescense, and adulthood. Thus, the most powerful principle in learning is that the child attempts to relate new to old. Once that is done, the next principle of Piagetian learning is to make the new knowledge one's own; to personalize it, to appropriate it. This appropriation process involves acting on, manipulating, transforming the object of knowledge. Learners often cannot relate to an event or a phenomenon that they are taught in school. Often the difficulty lies in the fact that the new knowledge has been so formalized (through symbols, mathematical equations, etc.) that the learner is unable to recognize it as something he has seen, done, manipulated, etc. These principles are interrelated and naturally lead to a fourth.

Educators must have a thorough grounding in the content of the discipline(s) with which they are involved. This is an obvious requirement for any successful educational method. But aside from the obvious, this knowledge is particularly useful in active education for it enables the teacher or the curriculum writer to do two additional tasks: (a) it helps in the analysis of the historical roots of the disciplines in terms of whether a given discipline was fundamentally developed throughout its history through the means of discovery, invention, or convention, or some peculiar combination thereof; and (b) it aids the educator in arranging educational situations in which the structure of a discipline can be reconstructed by the students. The results of the analysis of (a) determines the extent to which the educator can do (b).

A fifth principle of active education pertains to the role of the teacher. *Basically, the teacher's role in imparting knowledge should be de-emphasized, especially in working with children before the age of twelve or so.* The teacher's role is seen as that of a mentor, creating conditions that will lead to the spontaneous reconstruction of knowledge by students. Thus, whenever possible, the teacher's role is one of guiding students to reconstruct knowledge for themselves, as opposed to giving them, through various means of transmission, ready-made knowledge which they are to memorize. Teaching, in the more traditional sense of the term, will gradually assume more and more of a central role as students' interests and cognitive abilities demand. By the onset of the stage of formal operations, if education has proceeded as described in this book, students will demand verbal explanations, discussion, and debate for they now have real activities onto which to anchor these explanations.

Sixth, active methods emphasize the processes as opposed to the products of knowing. This implies that educators should concern themselves with the routes taken to an end rather than being solely concerned as to whether the end is achieved precisely or not. In short, the mental actions taken to arrive at a goal can vary, and stress should be placed on the attainment of a goal through various means. This emphasizes the point that learning to learn is as crucial an ingredient in the knowing process as learning itself. The emphasis on processes of learning ultimately leads to the development of cognitive strategies for discovering and inventing knowledge. In active education, the ultimate goal is to equip the student with tools for knowledge-gathering and knowledge-creating. Processes which assist the student to research, inquire, and find knowledge on his or her own are paramount in this method of education. Piaget argues that through active methods the student will not only have acquired content, which he or she will be able to retain, but the student would have developed a process for acquiring information that will endure for the rest of his or her life. In short, through free exploration and investigation, the student not only learns, but learns how to learn as well.

Seventh, active methods call upon peer interaction. The interaction of students with their peers is a crucial factor in the development of thinking. Students' thinking is often challenged as well as affirmed through such interaction. Piaget has addressed this issue both generally, in terms of the impact of society on thought, as well as specifically, in terms of the necessity for social interaction in the classroom. For example, he (Piaget, 1974, pp. 107–08) states that: "The human being is immersed right from birth in a social environment which affects him just as much as his physical environment." More specifically, he writes: "No real intellectual activity could be carried out in the form of experimental actions and spontaneous investigations without free collaboration among individuals; that is to say, among the students."

An eighth principle may be stated as follows: *active methods expand the concept of "curriculum" by providing the learner with abundant, varied, and life-like materials;* that is, "the relationship of the classroom environment to the wider context of the learner's life must be considered (Wickens, 1973, p. 190). Whenever possible, students should be given a variety of concrete (nonrepresentational) objects upon which to act. This principle applies to students of all ages, especially if the content of the knowledge which they are about to study is new to them. (It is often advisable to introduce adults to new phenomena by initially slipping down from the formal operational schemes (abstract schemes) to concrete ones. Once the concrete operations are developed, it is then quite feasible to talk about the same phenomena in more or less abstract terms. In short, representational presentations, which are a step removed from concrete phenomena, should follow active intellectual transformations on concrete objects, events, or acts. Here a personal experience may help to clarify the point.

In one of my learning seminars, a nursing student complained that much as she tried, she couldn't convey the concepts of diastolic and systalic actions in the blood-stream to a group of nurse aids. I suggested that she try to concretize these actions by placing water in a balloon and allowing students to abstract the actions of water. They quickly observed that as they squeezed the balloon, that it expanded in width (diastolic action) as well as in length (systalic action). The students had no difficulty grasping these concepts after that simple experiment.

A ninth point leads us to the following principle: *active methods are didactic, in the sense that they allow for free intellectual discussion and interchange.* One aspect of this interchange is disagreement or confrontation, which leads to the possibility for entertaining another point of view. Egocentricity—which is revealed quite plainly in sensorimotor but particularly in reoperational children—is the tendency to view the world from one's own point of view. Intellectual growth, speaking ontogenetically as well as historically, is characterized by progressive de-centration. With intellectual growth comes the ability to view a phenomenon from a number of points of view. Disagreements and honest confrontations can often aid this process of de-centration. Moreover, confrontations of the type we have been discussing lead to dis-equilibrium in cognitive structures, motivating the student toward the resolution of such conflicts.

While an aspect of this principle deals with conflict resolution, disequilibrium and equilibrium, the other side of this principle of free discussion is the obvious need for social reciprocity that each one of us shows. We need to know what others think about our point of view, our creations, our songs, our music, etc. No where is this intellectual social reciprocity more evident than during adolescence. Adolescents, equipped with newly developed attainments of formal reasoning, long to debate. They love to exercise these newly developed cognitive structures. In so doing, they manage to test their grasp of these abilities. Social give and take helps to provide the much needed feedback that confirms or rejects this newly developed way of knowing. Thus, dialogue is indispensable to active learning.

Active methods recognize the natural tendency in people to understand through constant organization and reorganization of their thoughts. This necessitates the educational technique of returning to experiences already explored, to topics already studied, with various quantitative and qualitative embellishments. This point of view is consistent with Bruner's theory of the spiral curriculum. A beautiful example of how the principle of constant organization and reorganization is found in Papert (1980). His Turtle computer, which is body syntonic (it can behave much like the human body so children who are learning to program it can begin by thinking about their own bodies and then apply those thoughts to the computer), is initially a physical "toy" that can be manipulated through a series of commands. The "Turtle" will physically move around on the floor as directed. As soon as the children are ready, they may transfer their skills of manipulating the "real Turtle" to a Turtle on the screen of a monitor. On the screen the little programmers can make the Turtle do what they made it do on the floor earlier, and through more sophisticated commands, they learn to make it perform feats that it couldn't do on the two-dimensional floor.

Another principle that must be emphasized is that active methods de-emphasize verbal knowledge in favor of operational knowledge. Learning by doing is an old adage; but we must remember that active methods stress self-initiated activity, not controlled activity. Hilgard and Bower (1975) state that, in a sense, behaviorists have supported and advocated this adage as well. This is true only in so far as the doing has always been under the control of contingencies that resided outside the learner. In the behaviorist world of education, the learner is active only in a reactive sort of way. Be that as it may, the emphasis here is on de-emphasizing verbal learning. This simply means that we must strive to reduce learning of formulae, of equations, of definition, etc. when these formalisms have no antecedents in real action. The mathematical rule "invert and multiple" is a formalism, and empty verbalism. As Nathan Isaacs (1974) has suggested, "an empty verbalism" is just that precisely because the child has no basis for relating this rule to his own activity. Learning by formula leads to *dissociated learning,* or learning that is not related to the self, not syntonic in any sense. Students often can cite poetry, the pledge of allegiance, even principles of physics without having the slightest idea of its meaning. Empty verbalism, dissociated learning, rote learning—all lack meaning not because they are symbols, but because they are not symbolizing actions.

A twelfth point that characterizes active methods is the assumption that all knowledge is related, hence disciplines are not compartmentalized and taught in isolation of one another, but related to one another whenever possible. This point, like many of the principles that preceded it, is related to the principles of open education (not to be confused with open space education). In open education, an attempt is usually made to relate a number of facets to a central theme that is being investigated. For example, a central theme such as "Colonial America" may include not only the historic, developments of the times, but an excersion into the arts, crafts, architecture, and music. Coupled with the principle of active participator, this unit can lead to field trips and demonstrations of art and music as well as the active participation in these tasks.

A word must also be said regarding the Piagetian attitude toward audio-visual methods, including the film. *In general, Piaget recognizes audio-visual aids simply as "accessories" to be used to augment the teaching act, but never to replace it.* Moreover, Piaget considers the visual aids as technologically sophisticated ways of propogating methods of verbal transmission. Thus, in cases where the efficiency of transmission of information is a key factor, audio-visual means constitute an advance on the traditional and purely verbal forms of instruction. But we must quickly return to our distinction between figurative and operative knowledge in order to put these methods of instruction in proper perspective. Clearly, audio-visual aids constitute means for the enhancement of the figurative aspect of thought. These instructional procedures should be used to instruct disciplines which do not primarily call upon the operative aspects of thought. As Piaget (1972a, p. 75) has said, "operations are not reducible to perceptual or visual 'forms' and that, as a direct consequence, the intuitive educational methods must remain very much inferior in status to the operative, or active methods." Thus, just as there is a verbalism of the word, there also exists a verbalism of the image. In both cases, the danger lies in forgetting the supremacy of the operative over the figurative aspects of thought.

Similarly, it can also be said that programmed instruction and teaching machines as well as reactive programs of computer-based education suffer from similar difficulties as audio-visual procedures. Once again, if the goal is efficiency, then these procedures may tgriumph over traditional means of verbal instruction. The psychology of learning used to create programmed instruction, teaching machines, and the simple-minded computer-assisted instruction (which in their reactive forms are no more than programmed instruction transformed on the screen of a monitor), stems from the behavioral model of learning. As we have seen earlier, this model has concluded that learning occurs as follows: a stimulus is present, the subject reacts. If the reaction is correct and we wish to strengthen that connection, we simply *reinforce* the reaction. We must *repeat* this sequence in order to create a strong and enduring connection. This is important for with this procedure, the reaction to the stimulus becomes automatic; without it, the connection will be weakened, eventually in extinction. Behaviorists define good programs as those that minimize the possibility of error on the part of the learner. In this way, good programs require task analysis; i.e., the analysis of the components involved in acquiring a given task. Following the task analysis the components are sequenced according to an "expert" in the subject so that the learner can move from simple to more complex features of the program. This procedure ensures that the learner will make the correct response to each step ("frame") in the sequence. A correct response is quickly reinforced by showing the learner that his reaction is correct. An incorrect response leads to a previous step in the program. It is no surprise then that when learning is reduced to correct responding, and teaching to the mechanical and highly material form, that the machine can be far more efficient than the teacher. The teacher shold therefore be encouraged about all forms of technological innovations in teaching for they have proved that they can perform the mechanical aspects of teaching efficiently. But even traditional education recognizes that neither teaching nor learning can be reduced to these mechanics. Once again, the teacher could be spared endless hours when the educational task involves practice and drill. The machine, the computer is perfectly suitable to these ends.

I would like to briefly expand on the use of computers in education. I believe that computer-assisted instruction must be viewed on a continuum of learner passivity-activity. What we have been discussing is the computer-aided methods which are nothing more than programmed instruction, lifted from pages of workbooks and transposed onto a monitor screen. This transformation is a transformation of form only, not a transformation of function. The learner is once again a passive reactor to a preprogrammed set of information. In cases where drill and practice is necessary or where memory of facts is the major goal, this form of computer-assisted instruction can be of undeniable service. However, where the goal of an educational episode is the development of the intellect, i.e., the development of the learner's spontaneous activity, a more interactive mode of computer learning must be considered. Computer-assisted learning which requires the student to think—make judgements, discover phenomena, invent solutions through his interactions with the computer—is in tune with teaching for the development of intellectual processes. Finally, at the other extreme of this continuum is the ideal of the development of spontaneous activity through the computer. Computer-assisted learning that confine the learner to making a choice from a multiple of possible answers is essentially a passive form of learning. As I said, it is of undeniable service not only the learning of facts but also in *training* adults to perform certain set tasks or procedures. In this case, the computer program is meant to program the learner.

At the other extreme of the continuum is the design of computer learning interactions which enable the learner to program the computer. This is the form of computer education that is most consonant with Piagetian learning, with the development of the spontaneous forms of human thinking. The central features of this type of computer education is the idea that the learners will make mistakes in programming the computer and that these mistakes will lead them to "debug" their own thinking in an effort to clear the mistake. This "debugging" process is central in Piagetian learning in that it forces the learner to make his own thinking the object of scrutiny, the object of the educational episode. Essentially, by teaching children a simple computer language, we can enable them to become little epistemologists, thinkers of their own thinking processes. This is precisely what Papert (1980) and his colleagues at the Artificial Intelligence Laboratory at the Massachusetts Institute of Technology have been able to do. They created a computer system which enables children to reinvent the principles of geometry or to discover principles of physics. Children can program the "Turtle" (a robot of sorts) to carry out certain functions. For example, they can make the Turtle go forward a certain distance, turn right or left a certain amount, go backwards, etc. In this way the children (6, 7, 8 year-olds) invent geometry, as when they create the shape of a house, for example, by programming the computer to go forward 100, turn right 90, forward 100, right 90, etc. Initially they have no idea that 90 refers to the geometrical concept of "degree," but as they command the Turtle to turn various numbers, they discover that 90 makes a right angled shape, and so on. Having discovered a pattern, they can quickly apply a label to it and relate it to a formalization which we call a "degree." In this way figurative knowledge is made subservient to operational knowledge, a Piagetian tenet which we have seen already. Turtle geometry as it is called soon can be transformed from the two-dimensional limitation of the Turtle on the floor to a Turtle on the computer screen which can be manipulated in three-dimensions. The screen Turtle can be rotated for example.

And so we conclude that computers can be of assistance not only in the learning of facts, not only in training, but also in developing the processes of reasoning itself. All this depends on our assumptions regarding the nature of the learner, the learning process, as well as upon the goals of the educational enterprise in question. Computers can help children to become "little epistemologists" if the children are given a chance to program the computer as opposed to allowing the computer to program them.

A final point addresses the question of attitude toward making errors in the course of learning and toward evaluation in general. It is clear that the emphasis placed on investigation guided by the teacher is bound to result in errors made by the student. Unlike programmed instruction which is designed ever so meticulously to lead the student to correct responses so that they are followed by reinforcement, *active methods accept mistakes as a natural outcome of learning*. Often one learns a great deal more from making errors than from responding correctly. For example, in testing hypotheses, mistakes often provide a great deal of information by eliminating possibilities. Furthermore, making mistakes is very natural to learners. Piaget has shown, as we have seen earlier, that the intuitive reasoning of a preoperational child is no more wrong than crawling prior to walking. The theories of the preoperational child (as in the case of my own daughter, when at the age of five she insisted that a car is alive because it moved) *are* wrong. But being wrong is better than memorizing a formalism that is right, but not know what it means! Thus, theorizing is understood as being natural in the development of knowledge. It should be encouraged. Children's theories about why things float (e.g., the size of the object), or what makes the wind blow (e.g., the leaves of the trees), or what makes the shadow follow them (e.g., the sun follows the child) are all wrong theories. Yet these wrong theories are necessary in the evolution of thought. To short-circuit the process by drilling "correct" theories is not the answer. To emphasize a point made earlier, active methods place a major emphasis on the processes of learning, not on reinforcing (rewarding) the outcome of that process. Thus, guidance during the learning process supercedes definitive evaluation at the end of the instructional period. Moreover, evaluation of student work is best achieved by

> the long-term observation of the students' work by the teacher . . . [and] if emotional elements of pressure and stress could be eliminated, [a second method] is the use of open-book examinations. This method allows the student to demonstrate his ability to engage in thinking (Patterson, 1977, pp. 118–19).

I should perhaps close by commenting on the single, most popular question asked by educators and psychologists alike. The question is as follows: "How can we accelerate the intellectual development of children?" In fact, in recent years a number of "educational kits" have appeared whose purpose it is to do just that: to accelerate the cognitive development of children by directly training children on the experimental tasks that were designed to assess the attainment of particular cognitive structures. These kits generally consist of objects that were initially used by Piaget and his associates in researching the intellectual competence of children at various ages. The problem is that these research tools have been converted into teaching tools in an attempt to deliberately accelerate children's conceptual development of a given phenomenon. This is obviously a mindless activity and reveals a lack of understanding of Piaget's theory as well as its educational implications and appropriate uses. Direct, short-term training is not likely to change the operative knowledge of individuals. As Duckworth (1964, p. 3) has put it: "Modifying a child's effective set of mental operations depends on a much wider, longer-lasting and fundamental approach, which involves all of the child's activity."

In short, the educator should realize that changes in mental structures are in part time-dependent. To change fundamental ways, intellectual operations require direct and logico-mathematical experience, social interchange, and time. Rather than spending time on specific training of mental operations, the teacher would be better advised to learn, by careful observation and one-to-one questioning, as much as he or she can about the student's level of comprehension of varous phenomena. Through such an approach we can expect to make education a truly constructive activity for our student.

A Final Comment

In and of themselves the implications outlined above do not constitute a total approach for the education of the whole child. It should be stressed that these implications are limited to the sphere of cognitive development, and while cognitive development is central to any educational endeavor, it is not sufficient. An education of the whole child must also consider other aspects of development as well: physical, moral, personal, social, and aesthetic. Thus, it is clear that an entire education cannot be based solely upon the theories and findings of Piaget; it must be founded on a more comprehensive structure.

It will be recalled that Piaget's notions on education are elaborations of an educational tradition historically espoused by Rousseau, Pestalozzi, and Proebel; by William James and John Dewey. Piaget has contributed to this historically revolutionary approach by providing the most comprehensive theory of developmental cognitive psychology known to man. This extraordinary achievement, when considered jointly with the philosophical roots of which it is a part and merged with other already-existing and consistent theories and practices, can motivate an education of the whole child.

One can point to a number of educational approaches which have been motivated by, consistent with, and influenced by the Piagetian enterprise. Among these are the developmental-interaction approach, (otherwise known as the Bank Street approach), and the world renowned British primary school movement, to say nothing of the numerous infant education programs and pre-school education programs as well. In short, Piagetian theory and related findings give rise to numerous educational implications from which one can extrapolate curriculum as well as teaching practices that enable the child to extend the state of society's knowledge. In the final analysis, we must educate our children not merely to repeat society's ready-made formulae, but also to discover phenomena as well as invent new ideas. Active education is aimed at the child's natural way of learning and knowing. This way of knowing begins by relating knowledge to what is already known and by owning that knowledge by using it. The Piaget imperative is society's imperative: society must transform its educational system into a form of education which makes active learning its central enterprise.

References

Ausubel, D.P. *The psychology of meaningful verbal learning.* New York: Grune and Stratton, 1963.

Bellack, A., *et al. Language of the classroom,* New York: Teachers College Press, 1966.

Berlyne, D.E., "Curiousity and education." In J.D. Krumbolts (ed.), *Learning and the educational process.* Chicago: Rand McNally, 1965.

Berry, J.W. and P. Dasen, *Culture and cognition: Readings in cross-cultural psychology,* London: Methuen Press, 1973.

Blackie, J. *Inside the primary school.* London: Her Majesty's Stationary Office, 1967.

Bransford, J. *Human cognition: learning, understanding, and remembering.* Belmont, CA: Wadsworth, 1979.

Bruner, J. *The process of education.* Cambridge: Harvard University Press, 1960.

Bruner, J. *Toward a theory of instruction.* Cambridge: Belkap Press, 1966.

Charlesworth, W.R., "The role of surprise in cognitive development", in D. Elkins and J.H. Flavel (eds.), *Studies in cognitive development,* New York: Oxford University Press, 1969.

Chomsky, N. *Aspects of a theory of syntax.* Cambridge: MIT Press, 1965.

Chomsky, N. *Language and mind.* New York: Harcourt, Brance, Javonivick, 1972.

Dasen, P. *Piagetian psychology: Cross cultural contributions.* New York: Gardner Press. 1977.

Dennison, G. *The lives of children.* New York: Vintage, 1969.

Duckworth E. "Piaget rediscovered." In R.E. Ripple and U.N. Rock-castle (eds.), *Piaget rediscovered*. Ithaca, N.Y.: Cornell University Press, 1964.

Elkind, D. *Children and adolscence: Interpretive essays on Jean Piaget*. New York: Oxford University Press, 1970.

Flavell, J.H. *The developmental psychology of Jean Piaget*. Princeton, N.J.: Van Hostrand, 1963.

Furth, H.G. *Piaget for teachers*. Englewood Cliffs, N.J.: Prentice-Hall, 1970.

Furth, H.G. "The operative and figurative aspects of knowledge in Piaget's theory", in B.A. Geber (ed.), *Piaget and knowing: Studies in genetic epistemology,* London: Routledge & Kegan Paul, 1977.

Ginsburg, H., and S. Opper. *Piaget's theory of intellectual development*. Englewood Cliffs, N.J.: Prentice-Hall, 1969.

Goodnow, J., and G. Bethon. "Piaget's tasks: the effects of schooling and intelligence." *Child Development,* 1966, 37, 573-582.

Gruber H.E. and J. Jacques (eds.). *The essential Piaget*. New York: Basic Books, 1977.

Hilgard, E.R. and G.H. Bower. *Theories of learning*. Englewood Cliffs, N.J.: Prentice-Hall, 1975.

Hunt, J. McV. *Intelligence and experience*. New York: Ronald Press, 1961.

Inhelder, B. and J. Piaget. *The growth of logical thinking from child-hood to adolescence,* New York: Basic Books, 1958.

Inhelder, B., Sinclair, H., and M. Bovet. *Learning and the development of cognition*. Cambridge, Mass.: Howard University Press, 1974.

Isaacs, N. *Children's ways of knowing*. New York: Teachers College Press, 1974.

Jacob, S.H. "Piaget and Education: Aspects of a Theory." *Educational Forum,* Winter 1982a, 221-237.

Jacob, S.H. "Piaget and Education Aspects of a Theory." *Educational Forum,* Spring 1982b, 265-281.

Jacob, S.H., and Deming, B. "The concept of concept: A transformational viewpoint", in Weizmann, Brown, Levison, and Taylor (eds.) *Piagetian theory and its implications for the helping professions,* Vol. 1, 1978.

Kitchener, R.F. "Epigenesis: the role of biological models in developmental psychology," *Human Development,* Vol. 21, No. 3, 1978.

Kuhn, T. *The Structure of scientific revolutions,* Chicago: University of Chicago Press, 1970.

Markle, S. "They teach concepts, don't they." *Educational Researcher,* 1975, 4, 3-9.

McKeachie, Wilbert J. "Instructional psychology", *Annual Review of Psychology* Vol. 25, pp. 161-186, 1974.

McNally, D.W. *Piaget, education, and the teacher.* Sydney: Holder and Stoughton, 1975.

Papert, S. *Mindstorms.* New York: Basic Books, 1980.

Patterson, C.H. *Foundations for a theory of instruction and educational psychology.*

Perrett-Clermont, N. "L'interaction sociale comme facteur du development cognitif," These presentee a la faculty de psychologie et des science do l'education de l'universite de Geneve, Novombre, 1976.

Phillips, J.L. *The origins of intellect: Piaget's Theory.* New York: Freeman Press, 1975.

Piaget, J. *Psychology of intelligence.* New York: Hartcourt, Brace, 1950.

Piaget, J. *The development of thought: Equilibration of cognitive structures.* London: Blackwell, 1978.

Piaget, J. *The origins of intelligence in children.* New York: International Universities Press, 1952.

Piaget, J. "Apprentissage et connaissance" (Premiere partie). In P. Greco and J. Piaget (eds.), *Etudes d'epistemologie genetique.* Vol. 7, Apprentissage et connaissance. Paris: Presses Universitaires de France, 1959a.

Piaget, J. "Apprentissage et connaissance," (Seconde partie). In M. Goustard *et al.* (eds.), Etudes d'epistemologie genetique. Vol. 10, *La logigue de apprentissages.* Paris: Presses Universitaires de France, 1959b.

Piaget, J. "The genetic approach to the psychology of thought." *Journal of Educational Psychology,* 1961, 52, 275-281.

Piaget, J. "Development and learning." *Journal of Research in Science Teaching,* Vol. 2, 1964, pp. 196-186.

Piaget, J. *Genetic epistemology.* New York: Columbia University Press, 1970.

Piaget, J. *Structuralism.* London: Routledge & Kegan Paul, 1971.

Piaget, J. *Science of education and the psychology of the child.* New York: The Viking Press, 1972a.

Piaget, J. *Principles of genetic epistemology.* New York: Basic Books, 1972b.

Piaget, J. *To understand is to invent.* New York: Viking Press, 1974.

Piaget, J. and Inhlder, B. *The psychology of the child.* New York: Basic Books, 1969.

Piaget, J. and Inhelder, B. *Memory and intelligence.* New York: Basic Books, 1973.

Scribner, S. "Modes of thinking and ways of speaking: culture and logic reconsidered." Unpublished manuscript, 1976.

Silberman, C. *Crisis in the classroom.* New York: Vintage, 1969.

Skinner, B.F. *Science and human behavior.* New York: MacMillan, 1953.

Smith, F. *Comprehension and learning.* New York: Holt, Rinehart and Winston, 1975.

Sprinthall, R.C. and Sprinthall, N.A., *Educational psychology: A developmental approach.* Reading, Mass.: Addison-Wesley, 1981.

Wickens, D. in Schwebel, M. and Raph, J. *Piaget in the classroom.* New York: Basic Books, 1973.

ABOUT THE AUTHOR

Saied H. Jacob is Associate Professor, Educational Psychology, at the University of Maryland-Baltimore County. He is the author of numerous articles, and has consulted widely on Piagetian theory and its implications for education. In 1978 Dr. Jacob spent his sabbatical leave with the Piaget cadre at the Center for the Study of Genetic Epistemology in Geneva.